BARNES & NOBLE BASICS™

getting into college

by Gail Hall Zarr

BARNES
& NOBLE
BOOKS

ISBN 0760733295

First Edition
Printed and bound in the United States of America

For information, contact:
Silver Lining Books
122 Fifth Avenue
New York, NY 10011
212-633-4000

Titles in the **Barnes & Noble Basics**™ series:
Barnes & Noble Basics *Volunteering*
Barnes & Noble Basics *Getting a Grant*

Title page: Two scholars, one symbolizing art and literature (right), the other representing the sciences (left), grace the entrance to the Pattee Library at Pennsylvania State University.

introduction

Everyone knows getting into college isn't easy. But who knew the process was so complicated? These days there are so many schools to choose from, and so many factors to weigh—like cost, location, career preferences—not to mention tests to take, essays to write, forms to fill out, and letters of recommendation to get.

The list of things to do is mind-boggling. Where do you start? By getting smart and getting as much inside information as you can. That's where **Barnes & Noble Basics** *Getting into College* comes in. It walks you through the entire process from planning, to choosing, to applying, to adjusting to college life. It connects all the dots and answers all your hard questions like: How do you pick a school that's right for you? (See page 18.) What's this "formula" colleges use to rate applications? (See page 74.) Who gets financial aid and why? (See page 146.) And what the heck do you do when you actually get in? (See page 178.)

Yes, getting into college is a lot of hard work. But it can be done, especially if you take it step by step. So relax. The right college is waiting for you. And getting in just got a whole lot easier.

Barb Chintz

Editorial Director, the Barnes & Noble Basics™ series

table of contents

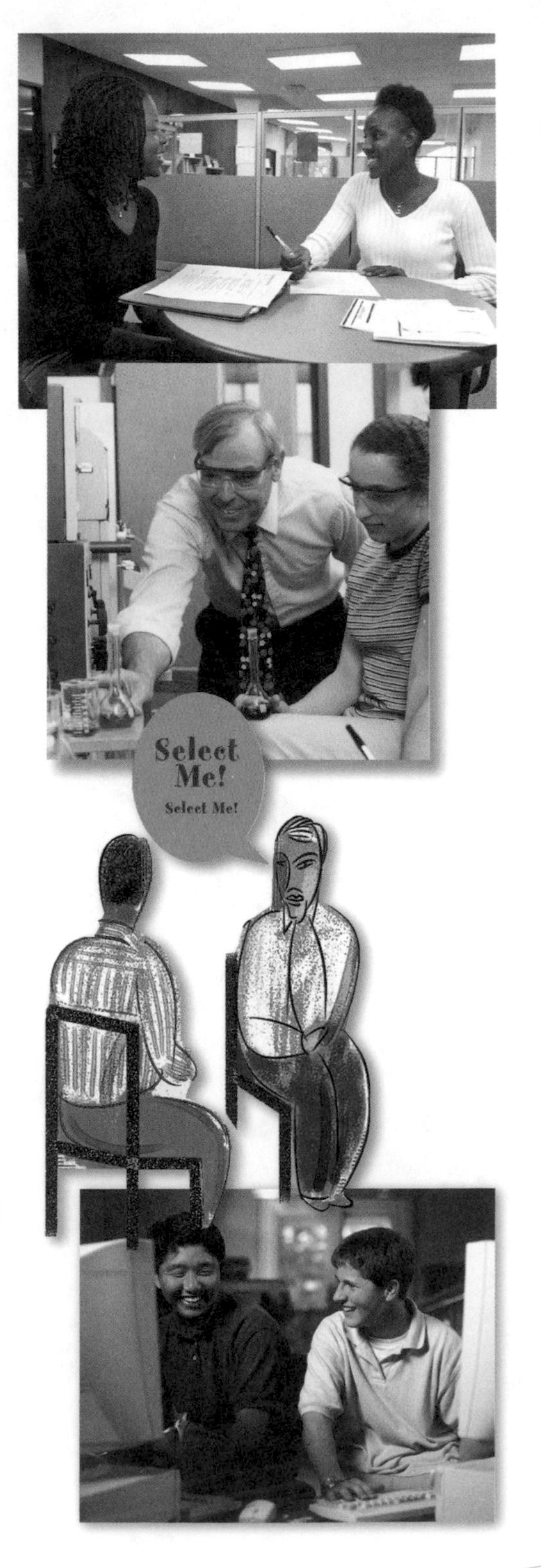

chapter 1

Is a college degree really worth the money?
Check out page 25

Getting started

planning for college

Relax! Your dreams are within reach

So you want to go to college. Good for you. Most people agree on the importance of a college education and the amazing influence it can have on what you do with your life, how much you earn, and how you learn to learn, a skill you'll value forever.

Despite what you may have heard about the rising numbers of applicants, stratospheric standardized test scores, and eye-popping price tags, it's still possible to get into a good, affordable college. If you keep an open mind and look beyond the hype, you'll find there are plenty of excellent colleges and universities out there that will suit your budget and your academic record.

While exploring your options, be sure to give yourself a chance to dream. Where do you want to spend the next four years? Ski country? The big city? Try on identities—start imagining your future. Will you be an architect? Dig for dinosaur bones? Direct a film? All of the above? Fine! It's all before you.

As Henry David Thoreau said about building castles in the air, "that is where they should be. Now put the foundations under them."

ASK THE EXPERTS

Isn't college outrageously expensive? How can average people afford it?

Keep in mind that the costs of college vary tremendously. While it's true that a small number of extremely select schools could cause sticker shock (total costs for a year at Harvard in 2002 hovered near $38,000), most students attend colleges that cost far less. (See chart below.) In fact, more than two-thirds of all college students face charges of less than $8,000 a year for tuition. Nearly half of all students attend public two-year colleges with an average tuition of less than $2,000 a year. And for colleges of all price ranges, financial aid is available from all sorts of government and private sources as well as the colleges themselves.

A Range of Choices

College	City, State	Average SAT Score	Tuition	Housing and Other Fees	Undergrad Enrollment
Community College of Philadelphia	Philadelphia, Pa.	Not Required	In-state: $2,770 Out-of-state: $7,750	Not Required	17,333
Temple University	Philadelphia, Pa.	930-1150	In-state: $8,062 Out-of-state: $14,316	$7,112	18,834
Penn State	University Park, Pa.	1090-1290	In-state: $8,382 Out-of-state: $17,610	$6,130	33,506
Villanova	Villanova, Pa.	1150-1320	$24,090	$8,330	6,892
Bryn Mawr (women's school)	Bryn Mawr, Pa.	1200-1380	$25,550	$8,970	1,307
University of Pennsylvania (Ivy League)	Philadelphia, Pa.	1310-1490	$27,988	$8,224	9,730

Information taken from The College Board (**www.collegeboard.com**), and reflects fall 2002 updates.

the parent-student partnership

Whose job is this, anyway?

With all the steps involved in applying to college, it can be tough for parents and teens actually to get started. Begin with a general understanding of what everybody's role should be.

For students

- **Determine your priorities**. You may be accustomed to letting a parent or guardian make all the decisions about school. College is different. As a young adult, you will face this as one of your first major decisions about your future. Start thinking about what you want out of college (see chapter 3) and, ultimately, what you want out of life. Forget about specific colleges. Know yourself first.

- **Communicate with your parents or caregiver.** They are your best allies in the college admissions process, and many tasks will require you to work together. So be ready to discuss your priorities with them, listen to their concerns, and work as a team with them. If you don't communicate, they can't help you.

- **Be prepared to do some work.** Do you want to control where you land? Then you need to be well informed about your college applications. Sure, you've got lots of homework and tests and extracurricular stuff, and applying to college adds up to a lot of extra work for everyone, but this is your chance. Do your share and you're more likely to get your heart's desire!

The Talk

Son

"I want to go to the University of Hawaii—beaches, waves, and sun."

Dad

"Hmmm. How will that help you find a job?"

Son

"The school has an underwater photography department with internships at the state aquarium. If I do well, I can get an entry-level job at Woods Hole Oceanographic Institution. If that doesn't work out, I can aim for a job at our state marine department."

Dad

"Sounds like you've done your homework. When can I visit?"

For parents or caregivers

■ **Share the decision making.** You'll have some serious concerns, like how much you can spend. But on other issues, remember that it's your teen's future, not yours. The final choice should be hers. Try to keep your emotions in check and be supportive, not domineering.

■ **Share the work.** You know your own child. Some children will want to manage this process almost entirely on their own, but some will need much more support from you. There are deadlines to juggle, forms to fill out, tests to take, visits to schedule—in all likelihood, your son has never handled anything so complicated. Like learning to drive, you both can do this step by step. Divvy up the tasks and monitor progress and compare notes regularly.

■ **Just don't end up doing it all!** Parents who wind up writing their child's college entrance essays are sending a message to their children that they cannot do it on their own. Plus, it would be unfair and unethical for anyone other than the student to do the work. Taking responsibility here is an important step for your teen in getting ready to live away from home.

■ **Provide some adult perspective.** The college admissions process puts a lot of pressure on students. It's up to you to help maintain your son's sense of self-worth. With so much competition, even the best scores and grades won't guarantee a spot at the most selective colleges. You both can aim high, but also include back-up plans.

■ **Be gently realistic about your child's high school record.** Don't obsess and make her more anxious about getting into a "status" school. Make sure she applies to a range of schools (see page 18), and never imply that your sense of her worth is tied to where she is accepted. If she doesn't want the schools that choose her, she can work hard and transfer later (see page 106).

high school timeline

Mark the calendar—what to do and when

January February

March April May

September October

November December

Applying to college means lots of deadlines, forms, and tests. Chances are you're coming into this timeline someplace in the middle. Don't fret about years past; just do what you can now.

Make a list of tasks. Talk to your parents about which you should do and which your parents should do. Pick a weekly pizza-and-plan night to go over progress on your tasks together, as well as review information and materials you've gathered from your research. Use this time to mark and update your calendar.

Freshman year

■ Meet with your guidance counselor and make sure you're in a college-track program. ■ Take the hardest courses you can manage. ■ Get involved in extracurricular activities that you like and stay with them through high school.

Sophomore year

■ **Fall**: Talk to your counselor about dates for practice standardized tests; practice the **PSAT/NMSQT** (see page 114) in math and verbal skills to prepare for the **SAT** or the **ACT,** admissions tests required by nearly every college (see pages 80 and 118). Consider **PLAN**, an optional test that can help you decide on a career or major.
■ **Spring**: May, **SAT II** (see page 120).

Junior year

■ **Fall**: Register and take the PSAT/NMSQT. ■ Make an appointment with your guidance counselor to talk about applying to college. ■ Evaluate your PSAT/NMSQT scores; register and begin preparing for SAT I or the ACT in spring. Attend college fairs.

■ **Spring**: Make a list of features you want in a college. ■ Begin research (gather materials, visit colleges, speak with local reps or graduates). ■ Develop a preliminary list of schools. ■ Take SAT or the ACT. ■ In May, take SAT II's for courses you've just finished, and any applicable **Advanced Placement** (**AP**) exams.

Senior year

▪ **September:** If you are taking SAT or the ACT again, register. ▪ If you are applying for **early decision** (an option to apply early to one school and agree that, if admitted, you'll attend; see page 16) or **early action** (similar, but nonbinding; see page 16), pay close attention to deadlines for tests and application materials. ▪ For early decision, you may have to fill out the College Scholarship Service Profile (**CSS Profile**, see page 149), a financial aid form. ▪ Check individual colleges' application and financial aid deadlines.

▪ **October:** Finalize list of potential schools. ▪ Fill out applications. ▪ Work on essay. ▪ Ask for recommendation letters from teachers and guidance counselor. ▪ Arrange for transcripts to be sent. ▪ Visit colleges if still needed. ▪ Attend college open houses.

▪ **November:** Register for CSS Profile (see September) if required by any colleges. ▪ Finish applications, visits, and interviews.

▪ **December:** Get the Free Application for Federal Student Aid (**FAFSA**). ▪ Research scholarships. ▪ If you receive an early decision admission (see September), you must accept and withdraw any other applications (see penalties on page 24).

▪ **January:** Make sure all application materials were sent. ▪ Submit FAFSA (can't be mailed earlier than Jan. 1) and any other necessary financial aid forms. ▪ Apply for other scholarships. ▪ Make sure first-semester transcripts were sent to all colleges.

▪ **February–March:** If you are still applying for **rolling admissions** (allows you to apply any time, as long as there are openings; see page 14), get all materials in.

▪ **April:** Review acceptances and financial aid packages. ▪ Revisit colleges. ▪ Decide on one college and accept, usually by May 1. ▪ Decline other offers. Find out deadline for housing application.

▪ **May:** Take advanced placement (AP) exams (based on advanced placement courses in high school). A good score in these tests equals college credit in many colleges. ▪ Start planning for a great year!

when to apply

Regular or rolling admissions

It used to be that everyone applied to college by a fall deadline and waited for an answer to arrive in the spring. That system, **regular admissions**, is still a common way of applying to many schools. With regular admissions, you have to be careful to meet the deadlines. Some schools, however, now have **rolling admissions**. With rolling admissions, you get a decision quickly—often within two or three weeks after applying. There is no deadline for rolling admissions applications, and a few schools even have openings in late summer for the fall semester. But it is truly a first-come, first-served scenario. Schools are filling up faster, meaning that fewer have seats left if you wait until summer to apply.

FIRST PERSON DISASTER STORY

I Wanted the Best

I wanted to go to only the best of schools. I figured if I applied to Harvard, Yale, and each of the other Ivy League schools, at least one would come through. What good are the stars if you can't reach for them, right? My grades were great, I was captain of the debate team, vice president of the student council, and involved with lots of other activities. But I didn't get into any of the schools! A friend of mine applied to a school with an early action policy—by early December she was accepted and knew if nothing else came through, she had at least one school to fall back on. She had told me to apply to a few schools where I'd be sure to get in, just in case. But I ignored her advice. I was devastated. Fortunately, my guidance counselor helped me apply to some other schools with rolling admissions, and within a few weeks I was accepted at a good one. Take it from me: Aim high, but have a Plan B!

—Sarah G., Boise, Idaho

ASK THE EXPERTS

What are the pros and cons of regular admissions and rolling admissions?

With **regular admissions**, as long as you meet the deadline you have a chance at getting in. All applicants are notified at the same time. But if you miss the application deadline, you are usually out of luck. You can apply much later to many schools with **rolling admissions**. If you have already been rejected by some schools, you may still have time to apply to a few others with rolling admissions. But move fast! You risk getting shut out if you wait too long. Even schools with rolling admissions often start filling up around May 1 for the fall semester.

Is a rolling admissions policy some sort of garage sale for substandard schools?

Not at all. While it's true that most of the super "status" schools still operate on a regular admissions basis and the more selective schools will fill up quickly, there are many good colleges and state university systems that have a rolling admissions policy. Some less selective schools do use rolling admissions to fill up their seats, but rolling admissions by itself is not a sign of an inferior school.

The ABC's (and D's) of College Rankings

Chances are you've seen annual rankings of colleges. For example, if you go online to the ranking by *U.S. News & World Report* you can search the list by different categories, such as the percentage of full-time faculty or SAT scores. But there are reasons to be skeptical.

A. With more than 3,600 U.S. colleges and universities, it's easy for an excellent school to be left out of the top 50.

B. Most of the statistics come from the colleges themselves.

C. There are top colleges, top universities, top private schools, and so on. For a complete picture, look at them all.

D. Most important, you may not care about the ranking criteria. For example, the percentage of grads who gave money to their alma mater is a measure on some lists. Is that more important to you than academic programs or location? Probably not.

early decision

And now, also early action

If you've known forever what school you want to attend, two admissions options might interest you. **Early decision** and **early action** programs let students who are sure that they want to attend a specific school get a jump on the process.

Early decision is for students who have done all their research and are certain they want to attend a particular school. You apply by an early deadline in the fall (the end of October or mid-November is common), and you may have a decision as early as December.

If you are accepted, however, you must attend that school and withdraw your other applications. If you change your mind, you may face consequences, including getting shut out of all colleges. Research any penalties before you choose early decision.

Early action plans are similar to early decision plans. The main difference—and it's a biggie—is that they are nonbinding. In other words, you can be accepted by early action and still take more time to make up your mind about other offers. Early action acceptances are usually sent out later than early decision ones, usually in January or February. You can apply to only one school using early action.

Many schools are rethinking the early decision option. Some, like the University of North Carolina, have dropped it, saying the early stampede filled seats with a less diverse group of students who had lower scores than those from the general applicant pool. So this move may not give anyone an edge much longer.

ASK THE EXPERTS

Some of my friends are applying under early decision. Should I?

Some statistics show that a higher percentage of students are accepted under early decision than under regular admissions at some schools. But choosing where to attend college is a serious, expensive life decision. Don't let anyone pressure you into making a choice before you are ready. There are too many good schools out there with seats to fill.

When is early decision a good idea?

If your academic record makes you a good catch for the school (ask your guidance counselor or the college's admissions office), if you are absolutely set on attending a certain school and don't mind giving up the chance to change your mind, and if you don't need much financial aid, you might want to think about it.

When is early decision a bad idea?

Avoid early decision if you haven't really looked at a lot of colleges yet, your grades aren't great and you need a good fall semester of high school to improve your transcript, or if you want to compare financial aid offers from all the schools that accept you.

I like the idea of knowing sooner, but is there some way I can land more than one school as an option?

Early action is a lot less risky than early decision. It can satisfy the itch for an early answer, and yet it doesn't lock you in before you really have time to make up your mind.

What are the penalties if I back out of an early decision?

Depending on the admissions cycle, you may be left without any college to attend. Colleges share lists of admitted early decision candidates with each other so that applicants can be withdrawn from the regular admissions pool.

how to pick schools

Long shots and sure things

When you start searching, you may want to create a preliminary list of as many as 20 to 30 schools that interest you. You can't apply to that many, of course, but it's a good exercise to make sure you know what you want and to see what you might be missing.

Most college counselors agree that you should apply to somewhere between four and eight colleges, settling on six as a reasonable number. Apply to as many as you and your parents need to feel comfortable. Six is a good compromise, because it allows you to apply, on average, to two **reaches** (highly selective schools), two or three schools at your general level, and one or two **safeties** (schools where you're guaranteed to get in).

Reaches are long shots, schools that are so selective that who gets in is almost a roll of the dice, even among applicants with outstanding records. Reaches are also schools where it's less likely that you will be accepted. Be ambitious, but realistic, about where you apply. It can't hurt to try! Let them know how much you want to attend, and see what happens.

Intermediate choices, or schools at your general level, are those where your academic standing and test scores place you right in the middle range of the students they accept. You have a good shot of being accepted, but you still can't be absolutely sure. Chances are you will be accepted by some, if not all, of these schools.

Safeties are sure things, schools where your grades and test scores ought to guarantee you admission, because you are in the top range for these schools. But be sure such a school is still one that you like.

Pick Some You Can Afford

Make sure that a couple of the schools you apply to are also financial sure things. These are schools you like and could afford, even if you get little or no financial aid. Some state schools, for example, are excellent bargains and nationally competitive.

Four good reasons not to apply to 20 schools

1. It's expensive: about $35 to $50 each time you apply.

2. It's time-consuming. You can't visit that many schools and survive!

3. You need to do your best on each application. If you are studying for college admissions tests, writing your essay, going on visits, and keeping up with activities, your senior-year studies, and all your other chores and special events, the quality of your applications will suffer. Focus on a few and you'll do better.

4. Even if you could, you would just be postponing making a decision, and it will drive you crazy when you receive letters of acceptance (ideally!). Don't procrastinate—prioritize.

finding colleges

Where to look for lists of schools

So where do you begin to find schools? Often, they'll find you—via mail and other means. But you can take control of your search in several ways.

Guidance Counselor Make an appointment with your guidance counselor (also known as a college counselor) as one of your first steps. Go armed with information about your academic record, extracurricular activities, and hopes and priorities for college. Your counselor should be able to help you come up with a preliminary list of schools.

The Web The Internet is an amazing tool for researching colleges. At Peterson's (**www.petersons.com**), for example, under the college search section, you can type in your criteria and the site will come up with a list of schools that match it. Many sites offer reviews, provide links to the college's Web site, and may have an automatic e-mail link so you can easily ask for literature from schools. The colleges' own Web sites generally give you more information than the fat packets they mail.

Publications You'll find college guidebooks, which are full of profiles of two-year and four-year colleges, colleges in the Southwest, the Northeast, Antarctica—you get the picture. One basic guidebook with profiles of colleges for the whole country should be sufficient, as for example *The College Board College Handbook* or Princeton Review's *Complete Book of Colleges.* Get the latest edition available.

Shopping List

Here's what to buy to start your college search.

Big planning calendar Fill in deadlines for applications and registration for standardized tests, plus dates for college entry tests, interview dates, college fairs. Mark when to start working on things, like your college essay.

One or two cardboard file boxes and file folders (legal size is best) You will be deluged with college materials! When you start receiving applications, books, and videos from colleges you like, you'll need a way to store them.

A good general college guide *The College Board College Handbook* gives profiles of just about every two- and four-year college in the United States. Peterson's, Barron's, Kaplan, and the Princeton Review, just to name a few, publish similar guides. Some of these same profiles are available online. Beyond the general guides, there are also regional guides and *The Fiske Guide to Colleges,* which gives in-depth profiles of some 300 top schools.

ASK THE EXPERTS

Should I listen to family or friends who suggest their schools?

Just because your cousin liked a school doesn't mean you will. At the same time, an endorsement from someone with firsthand experience is a good reason to take a look. Best bet: current college students.

What is a college fair?

These are events where admissions officers or representatives from many colleges gather in one place to answer questions and hand out literature to prospective college students. The National Association for College Admission Counseling (NACAC) sponsors lots of college fairs, even some that are online; check its Web site (**www.nacac.com**) for dates and locations. Your guidance counselor should have info about upcoming college fairs in your area.

Visit college fairs for up-to-date information about schools.

people who can help

Guidance counselors and others

Get to know the people who can help you be accepted into college. There are experts at your fingertips, from your guidance counselor to those you can hire.

The highest priority is working with your school's guidance counselors. Early in your freshman year, you and your parents should make a point of meeting your guidance counselor (or called college counselor, at some schools) and maintaining a relationship with this valuable source of advice throughout high school. Why?

- To make sure you are taking the right courses for the type of college you want.
- If you want to take honors classes, or advanced placement classes (high school courses that can provide college credit) later, you'll want to know you're taking the right courses now.
- To gain information about community service opportunities, summer programs, internships, scholarships, and fee waivers.
- To secure a great written recommendation and other help for your college applications.

You might also think about hiring a private educational consultant to coach you through the process, sort of a personal trainer for getting into college. The services, credentials, and prices of private educational consultants vary tremendously. The best of them are very knowledgeable. Some specialize, for example, finding schools for students with special needs, and in those cases their services can be very helpful. But they're by no means necessary for most families, and no consultant can guarantee your acceptance into a specific school. If you're interested, contact the Independent Educational Consultants Association (**www. educationalconsulting.org**).

Ten Ways a Guidance Counselor Can Help

1. Providing materials and helping with Web searches.

2. Helping you get started in your college search. They may help you come up with a preliminary list of schools, suggest paths for research, and help you evaluate your chances at specific schools.

3. Notifying you and your guardians about upcoming college fairs.

4. Advising parents on the college admissions process; they may hold meetings just for parents. Make sure your parents attend them.

5. Offering seminars for you on the college admissions process.

6. Reviewing your essay.

7. Writing letters to colleges on your behalf as part of your admissions packages.

8. Keeping track of test dates and registration deadlines; they may also have information about test prep options in your area.

9. Providing access to financial aid forms and answering questions about filling them out.

10. Helping to keep track of your admissions packages.

now what do I do?

Answers to common questions

What is financial aid?

Financial aid is money available for college students from the government, private sources (such as civic clubs or businesses), and the colleges themselves. It can make even very expensive schools affordable. A huge amount of money (currently more than $90 billion) goes out every year. Some of the largest offers come from some of the most expensive colleges. Even better, some of that money is in the form of grants that don't have to be repaid. So don't rule out your dream school until you see what kind of financial aid package it offers you. You may end up paying less than you would at a seemingly cheaper school. See chapter 7 for how to apply for financial aid.

I'm not sure I'm ready for college next year. Will it hurt my chances of being accepted if I don't go right away?

No, and don't force it! Lots of seniors aren't ready to head directly to college. Some feel academic "burnout," some want to improve their academic record by doing a postgraduate year—usually at a boarding school—and some just need time to grow up a little more, take a job, and save money. Most colleges view this "gap year" favorably, since it usually results in a more mature, motivated student. At some colleges, nearly one out of four students drops out during the first year, so it's not good to push students if they aren't ready. If you don't mind paying, there are consultants, such as those at the Center for Interim Programs (**www.interimprograms.com**), who will help you find interesting stuff to do, from culture programs in Nepal to working on a dude ranch in Colorado.

I was homeschooled. How should I apply to college?

Homeschooling is still so new that colleges haven't established uniform policies yet. Contact the admissions office at each one that interests you (a good idea in any case) and be ready to document in various ways that you are well educated. You may need a GED (General Education Diploma). They will almost certainly require you to take the usual college admissions tests, such as SAT or the ACT, and they may want you to take a number of SAT II subject tests as well (see page 120). The good news is that homeschooled children are accepted at even the most selective colleges these days.

Is a college degree really worth the money?

College is a solid investment. People with a bachelor's degree earn almost twice as much as those without one. That adds up to a lot of greenbacks over a lifetime. Beyond that, many people feel that one of the things you learn at college is how to learn—making it that much easier to change careers, or lifestyles, later on. Finally, college will introduce you to many subjects, friendships, and hobbies that you will enjoy and draw upon for your entire life.

Should I think about visiting a college I'm interested in?

College visits are essential (see pages 44–45). Start visiting colleges in your junior year, once you have a preliminary list. You'll be too busy to do it all in your senior year (see page 13), so take the summer before and plan a family vacation near some of the schools that interest you. Colleges sponsor open houses several times each semester, and most schedule informational interviews and tours daily.

Now where do I go?

CONTACTS

The College Board
www.collegeboard.com

College Is Possible
www.collegeispossible.com

Peterson's
www.petersons.com

Free Application for Federal Student Aid
www.fafsa.ed.gov

Interim ("Gap Year") Consultants:
The Center for Interim Programs
www.interimprograms.com

Where You Headed
www.whereyouheaded.com

PUBLICATIONS

Kaplan's Parent's Guide to College Admissions
By Marjorie Nieuwenhuis

Barron's Profiles of American Colleges

The College Board College Handbook 2002

Peterson's Complete Guide to Colleges

The Princeton Review's Complete Book of Colleges

The Fiske Guide to Colleges
By Edward B. Fiske

The Gatekeepers: Inside the Admissions Process of a Premier College
By Jacques Steinberg

Winning the Heart of the College Admissions Dean: An Expert's Advice for Getting Into College
By Joyce Slayton Mitchell

The College Admissions Mystique
By Bill Mayher

And What About College? How Homeschooling Leads to Admission to the Best Colleges and Universities
By Cafi Cohen

chapter 2

Which is better, a college or a university?
Check out page 31

Colleges and degrees

what's in a degree?

Demystifying those initials

Your choices are many—and just beginning! After you figure out what you want to be, use this list to find the degree you need and the types of schools that offer it.

Undergraduate Degrees

Associate Degree

A.A. (associate of arts) or **A.S.** (associate of science). Offered by two-year colleges. You can use the units in these degrees toward a bachelor's (four-year) degree. The **A.A.S.** (associate of applied science), **A.O.S.** (associate of occupational studies), and **B.M.A.** (associate of applied business) are degrees offered by **career colleges** (schools that focus on training for jobs like dental hygienist or hotel manager).

Bachelor's (or Baccalaureate) Degree

B.A. (Bachelor of Arts) or **B.S.** (Bachelor of Science). Awarded by four-year liberal arts colleges.

Graduate Degrees

Master's Degree

M.A. (Master of Arts) and **M.S.** (Master of Science). First you need a B.A. or B.S. Then you usually spend a year of full-time study in one area and write a **thesis,** a lengthy work based on scholarly research.

Doctorate

Ph.D. (Doctor of Philosophy) is the highest-level graduate school degree. It generally requires two to three years of coursework (earning a master's degree is optional), exams, and a lengthy written work of original research, a **dissertation**.

Innovative Degrees

Combined/Joint Degree

You can earn a bachelor's degree in three years and go to graduate school in the fourth year.

3-2 Program (or Liberal Arts/Career Combination)

Spend three years in an undergraduate liberal arts program and then two years in an undergraduate professional program, earning both the B.A. and the B.S. in five years. For example, Boston

University and Washington University in St. Louis, Missouri, offer this program through affiliated liberal arts colleges.

Dual Degree

Enroll in two departments and earn two degrees at the same time. For instance, students in the School of Music at the University of Michigan can also pursue a degree at another undergraduate college within the university.

Certification

You may need **certification** (status you earn after meeting qualifications) to work as, for example, a computer technician, or certification plus a college degree to work as, for example, a teacher.

Jobs and Recommended Degrees

Two-Year College Associate's Degree	Four-Year College Bachelor's Degree	More Than Four Years Various Graduate Degrees
Administrative Assistant	Accountant	Architect
Automotive Mechanic	Computer Systems Analyst	Biologist
Cardiovascular Technician	Dietitian	Dentist
Computer Technician	Editor	Diplomat
Dental Hygienist	Engineer	Doctor
Engineering Technician	FBI Agent	Geologist
Funeral Director	Investment Banker	Lawyer
Graphic Designer	Journalist	Librarian
Heating, Air Conditioning, and Refrigeration Technician	Medical Illustrator	Management Consultant
	Pharmacist	Psychologist
Hotel or Restaurant Manager	Public Relations Specialist	Scientist
Insurance Agent	Recreational Therapist	Sociologist
Medical Laboratory Technician	Social Worker	University Professor
Registered Nurse	Teacher	Veterinarian
Surveyor	Writer	Zoologist

Source: U.S. Department of Education, "Preparing Your Child for College" (www.ed.gov/pubs/Prepare).

university vs. college

Goliath or David?

After high school, you can go to either a university or a college as an **undergraduate** (a registered student not yet granted a degree) for four years and earn a bachelor's degree (unless you apply to a two-year school; see page 34).

So what's the difference? **Universities** are larger and also enroll graduate students. **Colleges** are smaller and usually focus on undergraduates.

Universities usually have lots of students and often have well-known faculty members, excellent research facilities, and a wide choice of academic programs and courses. However, in universities classes tend to be larger and the academic luminaries more likely to teach graduate students and conduct research than to educate freshmen and sophomores.

Colleges generally offer smaller classes, advisors who get to know you, and strong alumnae and alumni networks to help you with internships and career counseling. You may have more opportunities to get to know your professors and perhaps even do research with them.

ASK THE EXPERTS

I'm applying to a university that has a "College of Arts and Sciences." Is that different from the university itself?

No, it's just one part of the larger institution. Universities usually comprise several undergraduate and graduate colleges (Duke University, for example, has two undergraduate options: Trinity College of Arts and Sciences and the Pratt School of Engineering). Some universities have professional schools, too, such as law schools or medical schools.

Which is better, a college or a university?

Neither is better. It's a matter of personal preference. If you enjoy large classes, navigate new situations well, and like constant stimulation, a university may be a good choice for you. If you want a closer, more supportive relationship with a college community, you may gravitate toward colleges. Visit both and see what feels right to you. Also, keep in mind that no two colleges or universities are the same. Apply to a variety of schools.

FIRST PERSON DISASTER STORY

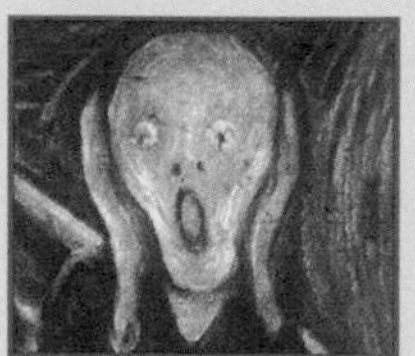

Loved the City—Hated the Country

When I started visiting colleges, I had a really nice time at this very small school in a rural setting. The campus was pretty, everyone was extremely friendly, and I felt good about the place. I applied and was accepted. But even though I was used to a big city, I somehow failed to notice how quiet it was and that everyone had a car (I don't even have a license). After about a week I was climbing the walls! The people were nice, but I knew this was the wrong place for me. I wound up transferring to another fairly small college, but this one was in a very big city. I got the best of both worlds and was much happier. Sure, some city kids liked my old college, but it just wasn't right for me.

—Seth S., Cincinnati, Ohio

public or private

A good education at any price

Just as there are public and private high schools, there are public and private colleges and universities. Public colleges and universities are financed for the most part by the government—in other words, your parents' tax dollars. Private colleges and universities rely on tuition, endowments, private gifts, and other private sources, such as foundations.

Public universities are usually much cheaper than private colleges. If you're looking at a public school in a state other than the one you live in, however, you may have to pay much more than if you were a resident of the state, so read the tuition information carefully. Besides being cheaper, public colleges usually give residents of the area an admissions advantage.

Because they are self-sustaining, private colleges are not subject to the whims of state or local politicians running for office, and many have proud traditions, strikingly individual characters, and long histories. And although many public colleges and universities (Berkeley and Michigan, for instance) are very prestigious, it's generally the private ones that some people attach status to: Princeton, Yale, Vassar, Northwestern, Stanford, Dartmouth—you get the idea.

Public universities, such as Penn State, receive government funding and usually are more affordable than private colleges and universities.

ASK THE EXPERTS

What are some examples of public colleges and universities?

Penn State, Ohio State, and Texas A&M University are all public universities. State colleges and universities often have one or two main, large campuses and several smaller ones in local communities.

Who gives more financial aid, the public or private colleges?

Generally, private colleges award larger—sometimes much larger—scholarships than public colleges and universities. But public colleges are usually cheaper, especially for residents. So apply to both and see which gives you a better financial deal—you can't know until you have an offer which one will turn out to be more affordable for you.

Is a bigger school better than a smaller one?

It depends on what you want to study and which school offers the best program. For example, if you want a career in agriculture, you might find the best program at a smaller, local college. Pick what's best for you and you'll be more likely to succeed than if you base your choice on the size of a school.

Do Ivy League grads have an edge in job interviews?

You can never predict preferences. One manager may prefer Ivy Leaguers while another may not. Your confidence, experience, personality, manners, contacts, the activities you pursue while in college, and how well you network and seek out people who can help you in your career usually play a bigger role. The Ivy League may open doors, but it takes more than that to succeed.

two-year colleges

New beginnings

Not everyone goes into four-year undergraduate programs. You may find it better to attend a two-year college. It might be that you can't afford a four-year college or you plan to work on your grades and transfer later to another school.

There are three types of two-year colleges: community, junior, and upper division. Students who complete their courses at community and junior colleges earn an **associate's degree.** Those who finish their schooling at an upper-division college receive a **bachelor's degree.**

Two-year colleges offer you a way to prepare for a four-year school or the job market.

Community colleges are publicly financed two-year colleges. They usually offer open admission, which means that anyone with a high school diploma or its equivalent is accepted. Most community colleges are also **commuter schools,** which means students travel from their homes to campus because there are no on-campus dorms. Community college will prepare you for admission to an upper-division school, for transfer to a four-year college, or for entry into the job market (many offer technical training).

Junior colleges are more like traditional four-year colleges. They are often private (although some state systems run junior colleges as well as community colleges), usually residential, and do not offer open admissions. Their costs are also more in line with those of four-year colleges. (Sometimes community colleges are called junior colleges, so check the detailed profile in your college guidebook.)

Finally, **upper-division** schools offer the last two years of undergraduate studies, just as community and junior colleges offer the first two. They are almost always specialized schools, focusing on career training. You must have completed two years of college to apply.

ASK THE EXPERTS

Is there any good reason I shouldn't just save money and go to my local community college?

This can be a very attractive option, but remember, you'll still need to figure out where to finish your studies two years down the line. Because community colleges have no housing, social life there can be stagnant. Many of them do, however, attempt to create a real college atmosphere and abound with clubs and social activities on campus. The key is to make a realistic assessment of the school: The best of them feature excellent teachers, small classes, and a diversified, motivated student body.

How do colleges transfer course credit?

Something called an **articulation agreement** between two colleges lays out the policies for transferring credit for college courses between them. These agreements make it easier for students to plan their coursework so that they are able to transfer credit from one college to another. If you plan to attend a two-year college and then transfer to a four-year school to finish, ask ahead of time whether your two-year college has articulation agreements with other colleges. In some cases, after completing two years you might gain automatic junior status at certain four-year schools. Make sure, as well, that you speak to an advisor at your two-year college before signing up for classes, to be sure you are in the transfer program and are taking courses that will be accepted for credit at other schools.

military academies and ROTC

A free education wrapped in red, white, and blue

There are five U.S. military academies: the U.S. Air Force Academy, the U.S. Military Academy at West Point, the U.S. Naval Academy at Annapolis, the U.S. Coast Guard Academy, and the U.S. Merchant Marine Academy. They are all superselective—right up there with Harvard, Stanford, and the like—and highly rigorous, both academically and physically. If you are accepted, your tuition is free.

The catch? Once you graduate (earning a bachelor's degree and a military commission), you will serve your country for several years. You also must decide well in advance that you want to attend, since you'll need a recommendation from your representative in Congress, along with top grades and test scores, peak physical fitness, and all the other requirements for highly selective schools.

If you are interested in applying, your best bet is to contact the academies directly for specific instructions—the earlier, the better.

U.S. Air Force Academy, Colorado Springs, Colorado
719-333-1110
www.usafa.edu

U.S. Military Academy, West Point, New York
845-938-4011
www.usma.edu

U.S. Naval Academy, Annapolis, Maryland
410-293-4361
www.usna.edu

U.S. Coast Guard Academy
New London, Connecticut
860-444-8500
www.cga.edu

U.S. Merchant Marine Academy
Kings Point, New York
516-773-5000
www.usmma.edu

ASK THE EXPERTS

What is the ROTC?

The Reserve Officers Training Corps (**ROTC**) is another way to pursue a military career while earning a college degree. The Army, Air Force, Navy, and Marines all run ROTC programs on more than 1,000 college campuses. While attending college, you take military classes along with your regular courses. While your classmates are lolling on the campus lawns, you can dazzle them with your uniform, military drills, and other practical training. If you nail an ROTC scholarship, it may pick up all your tuition expenses. Upon graduation, you receive a military commission and are required to serve in the military for a varying number of years.

Where can I find out more about the ROTC?

Look in your college guidebook for an index of schools offering ROTC. You can get some information directly from the colleges themselves. Also, check out these Web sites:

Air Force
www.afrotc.com

Army
www.armyrotc.com

Navy and Marines
www.nrotc.navy.mil

General Military
www.myfuture.com
www.students.gov
(Type "military" or "ROTC" in the search field.)

students of color

Honoring heritage

Historically black colleges arose after the Civil War to provide African-Americans with higher education opportunities denied them elsewhere. Howard University, dating from 1866, is a distinguished example, boasting many famous alumni such as Thurgood Marshall, Ossie Davis, and Toni Morrison.

Today, such schools remain a place for African-American students to find an environment where they are the majority, both in the classroom and in the social sphere; where there is a much higher representation of people of color among the faculty, high-quality African-American studies programs, and school administrations dedicated to the success of African-American students. For a list of such schools, go to **www.edonline.com** and select "black colleges."

For students seeking a strong Hispanic culture on campus, **Hispanic-serving colleges,** where at least 25% of full-time enrolled students are Hispanic, are a good choice.

For example, Texas A&M University–Kingsville is 65% Hispanic and a member of the Hispanic Association of Colleges and Universities (HACU). Established in 1986, HACU represents more than 300 colleges and universities committed to Hispanic higher education success in the United States, Puerto Rico, Latin America, and Spain. Although its member institutions in the United States represent less than 7% of all higher education institutions nationwide, together they are home to more than two-thirds of all Hispanic college students. You can find more information at **www.hacu.net**.

ASK THE EXPERTS

How can I tell how diverse a college is?

Most colleges provide a breakdown of their student population by ethnicity. Take a look at your college profile guide. You should see percentages of African-American, Hispanic, Asian, Native American, and international students. But more important, visit the campus and see for yourself. Check out the student center, look in some classrooms, stop by the dining hall, and if possible speak directly to minority students who are already enrolled. If classes about a particular ethnic group interest you, consult the course catalog to see what's offered.

How do historically black colleges compare with other schools?

Some historically black colleges, like Morehouse and Spelman, are on par with the top schools in the country. As always, the best advice is to consider a range of schools, visit them, and then decide what works best for you.

women's colleges

Defying stereotypes

You may find it hard to believe in an age of coed dorms, but it took a lot of struggle to make colleges coeducational in the United States. In the 19th century, women were ridiculed and harassed when they tried to attend lectures in male classrooms. And so began women's colleges.

Although fewer than a hundred survive today, these colleges include prestigious schools like Smith, Barnard, and Bryn Mawr. They have proudly held on to their traditions and attract some of the brightest young women in the country.

Among their benefits are small classes taught by professors dedicated to teaching, higher percentages of women faculty members than is the norm, women students in all leadership roles on campus, and alumnae networks that work vigorously to offer internships and career opportunities for their students. Learn more at **www.womenscolleges.org**, the Women's College Coalition, which represents 70 U.S. and Canadian women's colleges.

ASK THE EXPERTS

What are the advantages of going to a women's college?

Some research shows that women in women's colleges participate more in class, develop much higher self-esteem, and score higher in aptitude tests than women in coed schools. Women's colleges can point to a long list of successes. Attendees of women's colleges are represented in much higher percentages than women grads of coed schools in many important venues such as Congress, in high-ranking (and higher paying) corporate positions, and in fields that were once viewed as male precincts, such as mathematics and the sciences.

What are the Seven Sisters?

The term "Seven Sisters" refers to seven women's colleges founded in the 19th century: Barnard, Bryn Mawr, Mount Holyoke, Radcliffe, Smith, Vassar, and Wellesley. Vassar became coed in 1969, and in 1970 Radcliffe merged with Harvard. Although the rest remain for women only, Wellesley has **cross-registration** with MIT, Barnard with Columbia, Bryn Mawr with Haverford, and Mount Holyoke and Smith are part of the Five-College Consortium (along with coed Amherst, UMass at Amherst, and Hampshire College), with shuttle buses running among all the schools. This means you can enroll at a women-only school but take some classes at a coeducational school.

Is there still such a thing as men-only schools?

The number of men's colleges has dwindled drastically. Apart from seminaries and rabbinical colleges, there are only a few, such as the four-year colleges Hampden-Sydney, Morehouse, and Wabash, and the tiny, highly selective junior college Deep Springs.

career colleges

Butcher, baker, candlestick maker

When most people talk about college, they mean four-year liberal arts schools. But if you are already certain of the career you want to pursue, a specialized school, also known as a career college, is an option you may want to consider.

Career colleges may be two-year or four-year, and may be standalone colleges or part of a university. The main difference between these schools and a liberal arts college is that you will earn a different sort of degree or certification, and take most (or all) of your courses in your field of interest. Examples include business schools, teachers colleges, engineering schools, art institutes, music conservatories, nursing schools, seminaries, and other religious colleges. Other schools prepare students for careers in fashion, the health sciences, technical fields (including computers), agriculture, the hotel and restaurant industry, and more. Many community colleges offer technical training leading to certification or degrees in various fields.

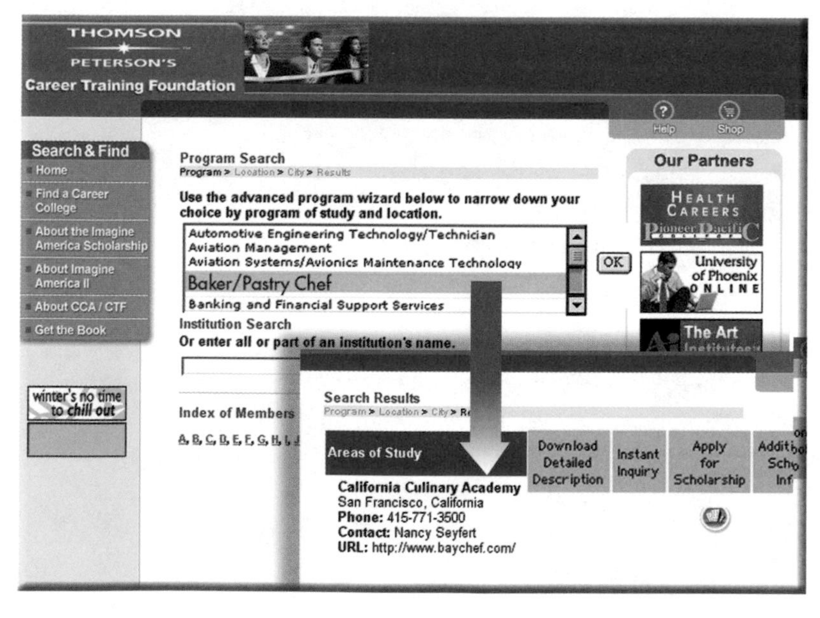

You can find lists of these schools in the index of any good college profile guide (see page 20 for examples). There are also specific career guidebooks, like *Peterson's Guide to Career Colleges*, updated annually, that give even more detailed information. Or visit Peterson's online at **www.petersons.com** and select "search and find," "career education," and "career college search."

The Case for Liberal Arts

Champions of liberal arts degrees argue that students who take a broad array of courses in the humanities, sciences, and social sciences are actually better equipped to succeed in their careers in the long run. They credit liberal arts programs with helping students develop better reasoning skills, along with the perspective and intellectual depth needed to deal with the complexities and challenges of a changing job market and world.

Attending a liberal arts college, with its huge course list, can be a wonderful, mind-opening experience. You may discover interests you aren't yet aware of, talents you haven't even considered (did you have a chance to study marine biology in high school?). So don't rush into making a decision about your career. And don't worry if you change your mind. College is a time to explore and consider your options.

Finally, a liberal arts education does not rule out preparing for a profession. On the contrary, many of the better-paying professions, like law or medicine, require you to first earn a liberal arts degree. If you want to do scientific research or teach at the college level, it's a given that you have to attend a liberal arts college and then go on to grad school. And many corporations recruit heavily from the ranks of liberal arts graduates.

visiting the campus

Up close and personal

Once you're on a college's mailing list, you'll usually receive lots of invitations to visit. But you needn't wait to be invited. Read about visits on the college's Web site, then call up the admissions office and schedule one.

Be prepared—stepping onto a campus for the first time is a different experience. This is your opportunity to see if it's the place for you. Campus visits can include an interview with an admissions counselor or group information session, a tour, sitting in on a class, meeting professors, and even an overnight stay. The summer is adequate if you must, but a deserted campus is definitely not going to tell you as much.

Attend college and career fairs in the fall of your junior year so you can visit colleges in the spring and fall of your senior year when colleges are in full swing.

ASK THE EXPERTS

What should I expect to see on a campus tour?

The tour should, at the least, include a freshman room or dorm, a dining hall, the gym, the library, and classrooms. Tours are often led by students and last about 45 minutes. Your parents should join you on the tour, but make sure you ask questions, and don't just take a back seat to them. *Tip:* If you take the tour before your interview, you can have lots of your basic questions already answered, leaving time for more substantive questions during the interview. Later, if you have time, stroll around the grounds on your own, check out the campus newspaper, and talk to students. It will give you a better feel for the place.

What does an "open house" entail?

Most colleges sponsor an open house each semester. These usually last all day and include tours, classroom visits, panel discussions, and opportunities to meet faculty. They may offer a chance to compete for scholarships. However, it may not be possible to schedule a personal interview on the day of an open house, so you might have to go back for a second visit. If that's not possible, attend the open house, because these occur only once per year or semester.

now what do I do?

Answers to common questions

People are always talking about the Ivy League. What exactly is it?

The **Ivy League** is composed of eight prestigious colleges and universities in the Northeast: Brown University, Columbia University, Cornell University, Dartmouth College, Harvard University, the University of Pennsylvania, Princeton University, and Yale University. Sometimes they're referred to simply as the Ivies. They were formed as an intercollegiate sports league (their teams still play one another) and have become synonymous with high selectivity and top-quality college education. It can't be repeated often enough, however, that there are many other high-quality colleges and universities besides these Ivies.

How can I decide which schools to visit?

Visit as many as possible, but definitely try to visit every school you are serious about attending. There's simply no substitute for the experience of actually being on campus and speaking with the people who work and study there. You'll be able to see the big picture and gauge how you feel in the midst of it. And if you aren't able to visit a school before you apply, you must visit it before you accept! This is a major decision—you owe it to yourself to really know what you're getting into.

What if I enroll in a career college, with its very narrow range of courses, and then decide that I don't want to be a ballerina, photographer, accountant, or whatever?

You've hit on the big drawback of career colleges. You would then have to enroll at a different college, and in all likelihood many of your highly specialized courses would not be accepted for transfer credit. If there's any chance you might change your mind, you should consider these options: 1. Enroll in a career college at a university, which usually requires more liberal arts courses than some of the more technically oriented two-year schools. 2. Enroll in a college that offers a liberal arts/career combination. 3. Enroll in a liberal arts college and decide on your specialty later.

How will I know if I'm good at or will like the career I choose?

Here's a tip: If you're considering a career college, try to get an entry-level job or internship in your chosen field before you leave high school. This will give you a better sense of what that world of work is actually like and if it's really what you want to do.

Where can I find a list of Hispanic-serving colleges?

Many college profile books provide lists of the roughly 135 Hispanic-serving colleges in their indexes. You can also search the online college guides, such as **www.collegeboard.com**. Visit **www.hispaniconline.com** and select the "top 25 colleges and universities for Hispanics."

Why should I attend a career college?

Depending on your goals and the type of career college you are considering, a career college can quickly prepare you for the job market (think a two-year technical school for graphic design or auto repair), put you among the most talented of your peers (think Juilliard for music), or provide you with in-depth studies and research opportunities that a liberal arts school might not be able to match (think Columbia School of Engineering and Applied Sciences).

Now where do I go?

CONTACTS

Preparing Your Child for College
www.ed.gov/pubs/Prepare/

Getting Ready for College Early
www.ed.gov/pubs/GettingReadyCollegeEarly/index.html

College Finder
www.college-finder.info
Information on career colleges.

Historically Black Colleges and Universities
www.hbcu-central.com

College View
www.collegeview.com/college/niche/hbcu
Information on historically black schools.

Association of Military Colleges and Schools of the United States
www.amcsus.org/

Women's College Coalition
www.womenscolleges.org
Information on women's colleges.

PUBLICATIONS

The Multicultural Student's Guide to Colleges
By Robert Mitchell

The Handbook of Historically Black Colleges & Universities
By Toni Hodge Kennard

Great Careers in Two Years: The Associate Degree Option
By Paul Phifer

All Girls: Single Sex Education and Why It Matters
By Karen Stabiner

The College Board Guide to 150 Popular College Majors
By Renée Gernand

chapter 3

How can I get an athletic scholarship?
Check out page 64

What do you want?

the right match

Narrowing your list

Make a list of the things you want in your ideal college. There are a few common criteria most students use. These include the quality of the academics, the location, the cost, the size, the athletics or other activities, and the social scene. You can find most of this in a good college guidebook or online at **www.collegeboard.com**, **www.princetonreview.com**, and other sites (see a list of books and sites on page 20).

Once you've determined your criteria, take a look at your initial list of colleges. Chances are, quite a few will drop out right away. They may be too far away, be too large or small to suit you, or not have the academic programs you are looking for.

Finding the Right College

For each college on your list, find it in your college guidebook (see page 20) and check the college's own Web site. Then ask yourself:

- Have I taken all the required courses for this college?
- Is my GPA (grade point average) in line with those of most of the students accepted?
- What about class rank? Am I in the ballpark?
- How do my SAT or ACT scores (marks in college admissions tests) stand up to their mid-50% range? (It's O.K. to be a little under, since this is the midrange, not the minimum scores.) The middle range at Pomona College in Claremont, California, for example, is a combined SAT score of 1,360–1,510, with an ACT composite of 29–33 for first-year students. (See chapter 6 for more information.)
- What does the college's admissions policy say about what they want?
- Do I have any special talents or qualities—artistic, athletic, or other—that might interest this particular school?
- Did anyone in my family attend? (If so, you are known as a **legacy**, and at some schools this will help.)

Remember, the test scores, GPA, and class rank are rough guidelines. Most college admissions officers bristle at the suggestion that they just "go by the numbers." If you have your heart set on a particular college, go for it and put together the strongest application you can. Ask your guidance counselor about recent applicants from your high school. As a backup, just make sure you also apply to other colleges where you're likely to get in.

Matchmakers on the Web

Lots of college-prep Web sites will help you find good matches (and they're a lot of fun to play around with). Another fun tool: at **www.collegeboard.com** (click on "finding the right college"), you can get side-by-side comparisons (size, SAT scores, cost, etc.) of three schools at a time. It's not a good idea to rely solely on these gizmos, but they're worth a look.

academics

Grading the departments, degrees, and faculty

Many factors will go into your decision about which colleges to apply to, but the most important to consider are the quality of the academic departments and the degrees offered.

Like many applicants, you may be undecided about a career, but that's all right. If you do have some ideas about careers you might want to pursue, then you want to attend a college that has majors (concentrated courses of study such as business, art, and engineering) that will take you in the right direction. You'll also want to know a bit about the faculty and how they work. Here are some of the questions to ask.

Academic Departments
▪ For which departments or majors is the school especially known? ▪ Is the school strong or weak in the major you want compared with other schools? ▪ What are the course requirements for the degree? ▪ What is the typical class size? ▪ What's the quality of the facilities—for example the library, science labs, dance studios, language labs, or whatever pertains to what you want to do? ▪ Does the school offer research opportunities or internships in your field?

Degrees
▪ What type of degree do you need? Does this school offer it? ▪ If you plan to transfer later, does the community college or other college have transfer agreements (see page 106) with other schools? ▪ Are you looking for any special degree programs (see page 28)? If so, are they offered in your intended fields of study?

Faculty
▪ What percentage of faculty members are full-time? Part-time? ▪ Are faculty members accessible outside of class? (Ask other students.) ▪ What percentage of the faculty members have terminal degrees? (This isn't as creepy as it sounds; it means they hold the highest degree possible in their field, usually a Ph.D.) ▪ Do professors—or grad students—teach most of the undergraduate classes?

Where to Get Answers

- Your guidance counselor.
- The profiles of the colleges in guidebooks (see page 20). Also, the more in-depth profiles in some books that cover just a few hundred colleges can be helpful (see page 20).
- Online resources, which allow you to search for schools by major.
- Admissions officers, career counselors, and students at the school—take time to get these answers during your visit, or call and ask.
- The colleges' own Web sites and catalogs.
- Word of mouth. Some schools are quite famous for particular departments; for example, Kenyon and Sarah Lawrence are known for strong creative writing programs. Ask your teachers, parents, and friends, but then follow up to confirm with your own research.

selectivity

How picky are they?

You may have heard the term "selectivity" in talk about colleges. It simply means how hard it is to get into a school. Although these days it seems that every school calls itself selective, some are way more selective than others. You can get a general idea by looking (yes, again!) at the profiles for various schools in your college guidebook. Look at two factors:

- The number of students who applied
- The number of students admitted

These will give you the percentage of students admitted. College guidebooks and Web sites do the math for you. For example, at the University of Oregon, a public school that draws the majority of its students from in state, 90% of those who applied were admitted. Harvard, a private school with an international reputation, admitted only 11% of those who applied. Why do you care how selective a school is? It helps you gauge where to send your applications so that you can apply to at least two schools that will most likely take you.

FIRST PERSON DISASTER STORY

Benched

Since 9th grade, I played hockey for my school team. My parents were behind me all the way. I made MVP two years in a row. When it came time for college, I was thrilled to be accepted at a big school known for its hockey team. I made the team, but I spent most of my time warming up the bench. Out there in a big college, there were just too many other good players, some bigger and stronger than I was. It really hurt, and I had to start re-evaluating why I was in college and what I wanted for my future. It's not that you shouldn't have the big sports dream, but sometimes your parents and the coaches in high school can get caught up in the fantasy. So go for it if you really want it, but have other options.

— Matt G., Deerfield, Michigan

What Does "Selective" Mean?

There are no hard-and-fast definitions of the levels of selectivity. But this should give you an idea of the range:

Most selective schools These are the hottest schools. Stanford, for example, pulled in 18,000 applicants in 2001 and accepted about 2,400, or 13%—fewer than 2 of every 10 applicants. The result is that Stanford can keep raising the bar on its admissions standards. For example, 99% of the incoming class had a GPA of 3.0 or higher. And you can bet that many of the students turned away have equally good high school records. There was simply no more room on the roster!

Selective These schools are known for high-quality academics, yet they admit a higher percentage of applicants. For example, in 2001 well-respected Hampshire College accepted 62% of its applicants and Brandeis University took 48%. But before you get too complacent, understand that most of their applicants were probably good matches for the school. These schools are simply not deluged with applicants the way the Ivies and a dozen or so other media stars are. Expect them to review your record carefully, and if your application is way below their standards, these higher percentages of admissions probably won't help you.

Less selective Some schools accept 70% or more of their applicants. They tend to accept lower SAT scores and GPA's and give more leeway to students whose high school records had some bumps. If any of that sounds like you, you may be pleasantly surprised to discover many fine schools among this group, such as Drew University in New Jersey, Northeastern in Boston, and lots of smaller colleges, like Lake Forest outside Chicago. These schools will want evidence that you are ready and able to do college-level work, though, so give your applications a lot of attention.

Open admissions This speaks for itself. Apply and you're accepted. Most community colleges have open admissions.

size and location

Choosing what you like

Colleges and universities range from an enrollment of a few hundred students to tens of thousands. Colleges are usually smaller than universities, but not always (Boston College has nearly 9,000 undergrads, about the same as Northwestern University).

How do you decide what's best for you? Check out the total undergrad population. For a university, you may also want to check the total enrollment of all its college and graduate schools, to see how the particular college to which you are applying fits in.

Before you make up your mind, visit a few schools of varying size. Although some people feel more comfortable on smaller campuses, others like the diversity and bustle of a big university.

Finally, look at class size. Do you care if entry level classes are huge—held in a movie-theater-style auditorium with hundreds of students? This is common at most major universities.

ASK THE EXPERTS

I'm thinking of going to a college clear across the country. How do I know if I can handle being that far from my family and friends? And how do I convince my parents?

Good question! Some guidance counselors say that early in the college admissions process, especially during junior year before students actually visit colleges, many teens think they want to go as far away as possible. But as senior year rolls along, many change their minds. Ask yourself honestly how you will feel if you can't go home frequently because of the distance or during the holidays, when airplane tickets frequently sell out. Ask yourself why you are set on a particular school. No matter where you go, you will gain a taste of freedom just by living away from home, even if it's in the same state. You may want to consider a school within a more reasonable traveling distance for the first year or two, then you can transfer to somewhere farther away when both you and your parents are more comfortable. But if your heart is really set, try to persuade your parents tactfully that it's the right choice, and consider their concerns—especially if they are paying.

Location, Location, Location

The location of a school can have a big impact on your overall college experience. Here are some things to consider:

- Do you want a setting that's like home, or are you looking for a change of scenery?
- How far away are you willing to go? (Better discuss this with your parents. Travel to and from colleges on the other side of the country can add up to a significant expense and lots of travel time.)
- Do you want to be in a large city, a suburb, a small college town, or a rural area?
- What sort of weather do you like? Are you looking for sporting opportunities like surfing, mountain biking, or skiing?
- How safe is the campus and surrounding area? (See page 62 for ways to assess this.)
- Do you need a car to have a life there? If so, is there parking for freshmen? What if you don't drive, or don't have a car?

student life

A visit is worth a thousand words

By far the best way to evaluate life on campus is to visit and talk to other students. Right away you'll get a feel for the place, what students do for fun, and the kinds of students who go there.

If you absolutely, positively can't visit, the more in-depth profiles in some college guides will at least give you an idea about the pulse of the place. The Princeton Review's *Best 331 Colleges*, available at your bookstore or online at **www.review.com**, even ranks the best food based upon student surveys.

Call an admissions counselor at the school and talk about campus life. Admissions offices usually have a number of students working there or in volunteer jobs. Ask if there is a student you could contact by phone or e-mail—they'll know lots more than the administrators about what really goes on.

The Search for Signs of Life

All right, do you want to make sure you're not going to be bored out of your mind for four years or kept awake nights by roving packs of engineering students? Here's what you need to find out:

- What is there to do, on campus and off? Do you like those activities?
- What sorts of clubs and organizations are available to join? Do many students participate?
- Are athletics a big part of the scene? Is that good or bad as far as you're concerned?

- Are there fraternities and sororities? Is this of interest to you?
- Is this a dry campus (many junior colleges are, because of state liquor laws)? Is this a plus or a minus for you?
- Do you need a car, or is there a college shuttle bus or public transportation to take you to the places you'll want to visit?
- How diversified is the student body? Is this important to you?
- Broadly speaking, what kinds of students are drawn to the school—arty types, intellectuals, jocks? Does the school have a rep for being left-leaning, right-leaning? Or is it so big there's a little of everything?
- Does the college expand its social—and academic—opportunities by sharing facilities with other colleges?
- Is there a big commuter population at this school? If so, is the place deserted on weekends?
- What can you tell from the student newspaper, campus bulletin boards, and the college's Web site section on frequently asked questions?

housing

Choices, choices

Most colleges today offer loads of choices about housing: coed residence halls, single-sex dorms, smoke-free dorms, substance-free dorms, honors dorms, sports team dorms, quiet dorms, noisy dorms, dorms with double rooms, dorms with suites housing six or eight students—you name it. Lots of colleges require freshmen to live on campus in dormitories. Check with the college of your choice on its policy. After your freshman year you will usually have the option to live off campus, or in a fraternity or sorority house.

Nonetheless, it's best to keep your expectations in check. Even the best college dorms don't exactly resemble designer digs. Most are very basic, probably smaller than the space you are used to, and you will almost certainly, as a freshman, find it comes with an accessory not of your choosing—a roommate.

Dorms have rules. Some colleges conduct periodic dorm searches, looking for fire hazards or evidence of rule breaking (like finding alcohol in a substance-free dorm), and there can be serious repercussions for breaking the rules.

Still, most students enjoy dorm life. Try to tour one at every school you visit.

Get a Roommate

Even if it's possible to get a single room, it's a really bad idea for a freshman. Forget all the horror stories about roommates—if you really don't get along, you will usually be able to switch. But the adjustment to college can be very disorienting—most people feel a little scared and lonely at first. Having a roommate (or lots of suite mates) guarantees you at least one or more allies as you find your way around the new place and start getting to know people. Wait until you're settled in and have made a few solid friends before you consider going solo.

Dorm Check

Your campus tour should include at least one freshman room or dorm, and you should receive a clear description of the housing options for your first year and thereafter. Here are some of the questions you'll want to ask.

- Are freshmen required to live on campus? (You should, in any case.)
- Is housing guaranteed for all freshmen? What about upperclassmen?
- Do most upperclassmen live in dorms? If not, where do they live?
- Do freshmen all live together?
- Is housing single sex, coed, or both? For what years?
- What other sorts of special housing options are there?
- What's considered the best housing?
- Is there a difference in price among the various dorms?
- What are the rules? Do they vary by dorm?
- What about food? How far away is the cafeteria?

campus security

Learn what's safe

Most colleges take the safety of their students very seriously. But this doesn't mean you shouldn't ask questions. Colleges can provide better security if every student is aware of what is, and is not, safe behavior on each individual campus, what security measures are provided, and how best to make use of them.

How do you find out? Ask! Your admissions tour guide, the office of the dean of students, the police, or the security office are all good places for answers to your questions. Security is usually a topic during freshman orientation, but don't wait until then to gain basic information.

You can also check out some sites on the Web. One good site is the Office of Postsecondary Education's Campus Security Statistics Web site, www.ope.ed.gov/security, which compiles statistics on reported crimes for thousands of colleges and universities.

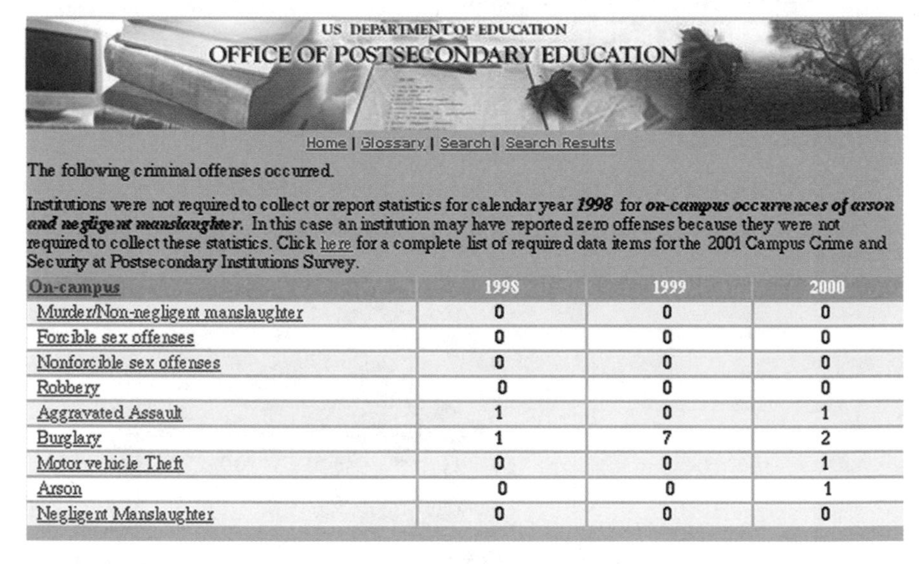
US DEPARTMENT OF EDUCATION
OFFICE OF POSTSECONDARY EDUCATION

Home | Glossary | Search | Search Results

The following criminal offenses occurred.

Institutions were not required to collect or report statistics for calendar year ***1998*** for ***on-campus occurrences of arson and negligent manslaughter***. In this case an institution may have reported zero offenses because they were not required to collect these statistics. Click here for a complete list of required data items for the 2001 Campus Crime and Security at Postsecondary Institutions Survey.

On-campus	1998	1999	2000
Murder/Non-negligent manslaughter	0	0	0
Forcible sex offenses	0	0	0
Nonforcible sex offenses	0	0	0
Robbery	0	0	0
Aggravated Assault	1	0	1
Burglary	1	7	2
Motor vehicle Theft	0	0	1
Arson	0	0	1
Negligent Manslaughter	0	0	0

Check out the student and local newspapers, and talk to students and residence hall advisors when you visit the campus to see if there are any serious concerns.

Any report about crime can be scary. To help put the crime rate of your prospective college campus or neighborhood in perspective, compare the level of crime at the school you're considering with the crime rate in your own neighborhood or that of your high school. Then you can measure the difference, if any, and decide how safe you'd feel living there during college.

Security Check

Here's what to know before you go:

- How large is the campus security force?
- How are they identified? Look around during your tour. Are they a visible presence?
- Is the campus well lit?
- Are there lots of easily recognizable, working emergency phones around campus?
- Is there an escort service for late at night?
- Is there transportation around campus? If so, what is its schedule, and where do you pick it up? Do many students use it?
- What are the campus crime statistics for the past few years? Have they gone up or down? How do they compare with other campuses?
- Are there safety seminars, especially for new students?
- What is it like off campus? Are any particular neighborhoods unsafe? Where do most students go when they leave campus? How do they get there? Is any form of transportation considered unsafe?
- Must you show an ID to enter a dorm? If not, how are the entrances secured?
- Do security personnel patrol the dorms at night?
- What is the crime rate or security level of the surrounding community?

college athletics

Getting the score

College athletics is a big world. If you are interested in participating, you need to familiarize yourself with that world early on in high school. Speak to your guidance counselor and your coach about your interests, your potential for landing a scholarship, which schools might be likely prospects, and how the rules governing recruiting and scholarships work. It's a big subject, one both you and your parents need to learn about.

Most colleges belong to one of three athletic associations: the NCAA, NAIA, and NJCAA. The associations set rules for recruitment, scholarship amounts, and minimum academic standards. Each association has its own rules.

The **National College Athletic Association**'s (**www.ncaa.org**) more than 900 member schools are grouped into three divisions. **Division I** schools are the most athletically competitive and include schools such as UCLA. Almost all offer athletic scholarships. **Division II** schools are also allowed to award athletic scholarships. They include schools such as the University of Nebraska at Omaha. **Division III** schools, which tend to be smaller, such as Concordia University in Wisconsin, must base scholarships on financial need.

More than 300 schools belong to the **National Association of Intercollegiate Athletics** (**www.naia.org**). In general, the NAIA is seen as less competitive athletically than the NCAA.

With more than 500 members, the **National Junior College Athletic Association** (**www.njcaa.org**) governs athletic programs at many two-year colleges.

The College Athletics Game

Here's what you need to do to win:

- Make sure you and your parents understand the rules governing athletics. Go to the Web site for the association or division for the schools you're considering (see previous page) and read the rules.

- Get a reasonable, honest assessment from your coach about your level of play, then look into schools at that level. Talented athletes are attractive to most colleges, so let the admissions officers know that you want to play, and arrange meetings with their coaches. At this meeting, provide evidence of your talent—a video of your winning point, news clippings, a résumé—and don't forget your transcript.

- If you win a scholarship, it's usually for one year only, with some exceptions for the most sought-after athletes. You must reapply year by year.

- Most important, no matter how good you are, don't neglect academics. You're right to want to follow your dreams, but only a tiny fraction of college athletes makes it into professional play, and most of them play for only a few years. If you're injured, your career can be over in a moment.

special-needs support

Beyond all barriers

If you are deaf or use a wheelchair or have some other physical disability, or if you have a learning disability (LD) or attention deficit disorder (ADD), most colleges will help you make the most of your college years. But the level of support and services varies tremendously.

Federal law requires colleges to provide reasonable accommodations and academic adjustments to ensure your access to an education. What's considered reasonable depends on the college. It could include a disability services office or learning resource center where students benefit from individual tutors, study skills classes, special testing accommodations, and peer study groups. These offices also coordinate classroom accommodations for those with visual, speech, and hearing impairments. You may find hydraulic lift-equipped shuttle vans to accommodate wheelchairs, as well as housing equipped for hearing- and visually impaired students.

Research and visit each college to gain a full sense of how supportive the atmosphere is, what kind of accommodations you can expect, and where you will feel most comfortable.

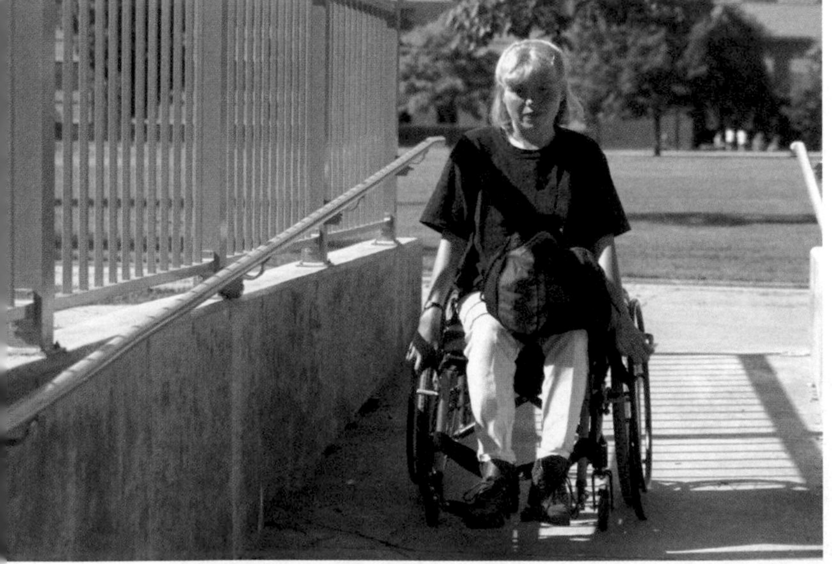

Once enrolled, you will have to supply extra documentation in order to be eligible for services. Often, it may take months to process the paperwork, so plan to start early. Discuss your school's specific requirements with an admissions officer.

ASK THE EXPERTS

Will it hurt my chances of admission if I tell the college I have an LD?

Not all students reveal their LD during the application process, and it's not required. It's only after you are admitted and request services that you'll need to disclose this. By law, colleges cannot discriminate in admissions decisions against students with disabilities. But they can hold these students to the same academic standards as the rest of the student population. Remember, the goal is not just to be accepted at a college but to succeed there. One of your main tasks will be to seek out colleges where there is academic and personal support. Some colleges are known for the quality of these services. Read, go online, talk to guidance counselors, perhaps make use of consultants, and when you have a list of colleges that seem promising, speak to their admissions officers and, most important, interview the student disabilities office.

Special Needs Resources

There is a lot of information available about support for students with special needs.

The National Clearinghouse on Postsecondary Education for Individuals with Disabilities is a great resource (800-544-3284 or **www.health-resource-center.org**) for college-bound students with disabilities. It provides specific information (and its own publications) about applying to colleges, links for further research, and it even profiles summer transition programs that can help make your college years a success.

Also, try these books:

Learning How to Learn: Getting Into and Surviving College When You Have a Learning Disability, by Joyanne Cobb.

The K & W Guide to Colleges for Students with Learning Disabilities or Attention Deficit Disorders, by Marybeth Kravets and Imy F. Wax.

Peterson's Colleges with Programs for Students with Learning Disabilities, by Charles T. Mangrum II and Stephen S. Strichart.

While these resources will certainly be sufficient to locate many good schools, you or your family may wish to pay a consultant to steer you in the right direction. Contact the IECA, the Independent Educational Consultants Association, for a list of consultants who specialize in college-bound students with special needs (**www.educationalconsulting.org**).

studying abroad

Tuscan sunsets, croissants by the Seine

While it's unlikely that you will choose your school for its study-abroad programs, they can be the icing on the cake. Or, if you will, the jam on the scone if you're biking around Cambridge.

This may sound like a fantasy, but in fact many colleges offer truly fabulous opportunities to study abroad. If you've got a dose of wanderlust in you, ask about these special programs and see what's offered. Review any extra costs and your ability to pay them. Usually, you go abroad in your junior year for one or two semesters. Summer programs are also available.

Sometimes eligibility for these programs is linked to certain majors, and occasionally the programs are linked to the study of foreign languages or cultures. If you have a real interest in a particular program, check out its requirements.

Talk with the school's admissions counselors about what kinds of programs are available at schools that interest you. Also, once you enroll, don't forget to keep track of the deadlines for applying.

ASK THE EXPERTS

What's the point of studying abroad?

Studying abroad can exponentially increase the educational value of a college major. It's one thing to read a book about Renaissance art and architecture, another to walk the streets of Florence and be surrounded by it. Similarly, if you are studying Russian, spending a semester in St. Petersburg will rapidly advance your progress in the language while giving you in-depth exposure to the culture and people.

How much will it cost?

Policies vary, so check with the individual college. Sometimes the cost is based upon a semester at your school, but there may be additional fees, and you'll likely have to pick up the cost of airfare. Find out if your financial aid package will travel with you.

What other kinds of special programs are available?

Many colleges team up to improve the opportunities for special programs for their students. For example, the Great Lakes Colleges Association, made up of 12 Midwestern schools (including Antioch, Kenyon, and Oberlin), offers all its students access to a globe-trotting array of programs based in Scotland, Africa, and Japan. Another well-known program is Semester at Sea, where students take a variety of courses while cruising to various points around the world. It's run by the University of Pittsburgh. Many colleges will accept its courses for credit. Another, sponsored by American University, is called Washington Semester and provides exposure to the federal government for students with high GPA's from affiliated schools.

now what do I do?

Answers to common questions

What about cost? Isn't that a factor in figuring out which college is right for me?

Ultimately, cost will be a big factor. But until you know how much financial aid you're eligible for, you can't know what the real cost of any particular school may be. You might apply to a state school, only to find out that the really expensive private college gave you so much scholarship money that its actual cost would have been less than the state school. When you make up your list, include a couple of schools you can afford even without financial aid—these are financial "safeties." But don't take any school off your list because of cost until you see the financial aid package. Everything relating to the cost of college is covered in much more detail in chapter 7.

How can I know how accessible the faculty is at a given school?

The best way to find out is to visit and ask students yourself. Another way is to read some of the in-depth guides (see page 20). The big, dictionary-sized guidebooks are great for general, basic information about each school to get you started. But read as much as possible about each school. You don't have to buy all the books—your guidance counselor's office should have many of them. See page 71 for a couple of suggestions. Generally, faculty at colleges teach undergraduates more than at universities, where grad students may handle many teaching duties to allow faculty to conduct research. But some small colleges are part of larger universities and can give you the same intimate feel and small classroom experience, along with very involved faculty. You have to be a bit of a detective and really listen for the gossip on the street.

Will studying abroad hurt my chances of admission to graduate school?

On the contrary, studying abroad is something done by the more outstanding students, who have the skills and initiative to do well in a different country, sometimes using another language and living in a generally less supervised situation. Assuming you do well, these programs should be an asset to your transcript.

I'm not sure what I want. Are there any of those self-evaluation tools or quizzes to help me figure out if I'd do better in a small or big school, or in the city or in a rural setting?

One you could try is at Peterson's Web site (**www.petersons.com/ugchannel/articles/selfevaluate.asp**), where there is an article by Charlotte Thomas titled "When Looking for a College, Start by Looking at Yourself."

Now where do I go?

CONTACTS

National Center for Education Statistics
www.nces.ed.gov/ipeds/cool

The NCAA 2001-2002 Guide for the College-Bound Athlete
www.ncaa.org/eligibility/cbsa

The NCAA Clearinghouse
www.ncaaclearinghouse.net

COLLEGE PREP

Peterson's
www.petersons.com

The Princeton Review
www.review.com

The College Board
www.collegeboard.com

PUBLICATIONS

The Insider's Guide to the Colleges
By the staff of the *Yale Daily News*

The Princeton Review's Best 331 Colleges

The College Board College Handbook

The Princeton Review Complete Book of Colleges

Barron's Profiles of American Colleges

Peterson's Colleges with Programs for Students with Learning Disabilities
By Charles T. Mangrum II and Stephen S. Strichart

The K & W Guide to Colleges for the Learning Disabled
By Marybeth Kravets and Imy F. Wax

Advising Student Athletes Through the College Recruitment Process: A Complete Guide for Counselors, Coaches and Parents
By Michael D. Koehler

chapter 4

Is there a formula for a successful admissions application?
Check out page 74

What colleges want

"the formula"

How colleges assess students

Is there a formula for a successful admissions application? Most colleges would say they look for key criteria.

- A high **GPA** (grade point average).

- Evidence that you've challenged yourself academically. (Did you take the hardest courses offered? Honors? AP's? That will be expected at the most selective schools, but not at others.)

- **Class rank** Where you stand in relation to the total number of students in your class, based on grades.

- **Scores** Your scores on standardized college admissions tests.

- **Résumé** Did you participate consistently in an extracurricular activity? Show any unusual achievements? Perform community service? Work? Anything outstanding about any of this? Do you have any special talents? What will make you different from the rest?

- **Application** The quality of your application, which is covered on page 92. This will include how well you write your essay and the impression you make during an interview.

- **The mix** Schools may have admissions goals that have nothing to do with you. If they are looking to strengthen their math department, for example, they might accept a higher percentage of potential math majors in a given year. They may be looking for more ethnic diversity or soccer champs or flute players or more people from Kansas for geographic balance. You won't know, so you just have to put yourself and your talents out where they can see them and hope they work in your favor.

- **Legacy** If you are a **legacy** applicant, which means that at least one of your family members attended the college, you may have an edge. Parents are the most helpful connection.

ASK THE EXPERTS

I've heard that some colleges award points for things like your GPA (grade point average). Is that true?

Systems vary, but many colleges assign a rank to academics from 1 to 9; extracurricular activities from 1 to 5, and personal qualities from 1 to 3. Your courses and grades will be evaluated by readers who are familiar with your school and geographic area. Extra points may be added if you have taken honors or Advanced Placement courses in areas outside your strengths, for example, math and science whizzes who take AP Art History. See more about admissions formulas at the Web site **www.myFootpath.com** (click on "Honors, AP, IB courses, do you really need them?").

My school is on a 7.0 GPA system, but most schools are on a 4.0 system. How does that affect my college application?

Don't worry, some colleges recalculate GPA's so that they are standardized from school to school. Others will look at your GPA within the context of your school and its grading scale. Go for great grades and the colleges will take care of the rest!

I played sports at my school, but I'm not a star athlete. Will it help my application anyway?

Yes. It shows that you can be a team player. You won't get an athletic scholarship, but colleges recognize how much sacrifice is involved in playing high school sports, considering the demands on your time. School sports are considered character-building, so by all means put your activities on your application.

high school classes

Hard, harder, hardest

Experts and admissions officers generally agree that the single most important factor in college admissions is your high school record. How much did you challenge yourself academically? How well did you handle those challenges?

Some colleges have a required number of courses in each subject that you must have taken in high school. This is the college preparatory program, or college track program, which usually includes four years of English and three or four years of math, science (including some labs), a language, and history.

Beyond those requirements, your school may offer honors or **Advanced Placement** (**AP**) courses (college-level courses for college credit). AP classes are usually offered in your junior or senior year, after you complete the basic requirements. Check to see if your school is among those where you can begin AP classes as early as your freshman or sophomore year. Selective colleges expect you to take the most challenging courses offered—or explain why you didn't. So definitely plan to take these demanding classes if you can handle them.

ASK THE EXPERTS

How exactly do Advanced Placement courses work?

AP's are rigorous college-level courses (now offered in 35 subjects) developed and administered through the College Board, with a set curriculum that is the same in every high school in which they are offered. In May, students who have taken AP classes take standardized exams. Students who receive a high enough score are eligible at most colleges to receive college credit.

What if my school doesn't offer AP classes?

Don't worry. Just take the most challenging courses your school offers. That's what colleges want to see. They're aware that not everyone has access to AP courses. You could try taking the AP exam without taking the course, but you'd have to take on a lot of independent study. No one expects that.

But what if I only get a B in an AP course, when I could have gotten an A in a regular course?

As long as you earn a respectable B, it's better to take the AP, in the eyes of most admissions officers. However, if you really can't handle the coursework, you are better off being realistic and taking classes within the level of your ability. Really poor grades will hurt.

your transcript

Give it your best shot

Besides looking at what classes you take, colleges also look at how you did in them. The most common way they do this is by looking at your **GPA** (grade point average).

Most schools compute the GPA by a formula that generally works like this: each grade on your transcript is assigned a value (A = 4 points, B = 3 points, C = 2 points, D = 1 point, F = 0) and the average is computed, taking into account how many course hours or credit hours each course was worth. Some high schools grade on the 7.0 scale (with 7 as the highest grade), which changes the way the GPA is computed.

Don't worry if your school uses a different scale, or doesn't award extra points for honors courses. College admissions officers often throw out the GPA's reported by high schools and recalculate your GPA from your raw grades, according to their own formula.

Another way of evaluating you is your **class rank**. Out of the total number of students in your class, where do you stand academically? Usually, this statistic is presented as a percentile; for example, the top 10% of your class, or the top 25%. Some schools assign class rank, but others don't.

Colleges get grade information by asking for it as a requirement in applications (see more about applications on page 90). You will ask your records office to send a **transcript**, the official record of your high school grades, directly to the colleges on your list. To prevent tampering, colleges do not accept copies.

Admissions Myths

Myth: I'm not in the top half of my class, so I should forget about applying to most colleges.

Reality: Grades and class rank are important, but if you look at the freshman profiles for many colleges you'll see that a lot of them accept students below the top quarter, or even top half, of their class. Use these statistics as a rough guide. They can give you some realistic sense of where you have the best chances at being accepted. If you can, show a pattern of steady improvement or some special talents.

Myth: It's smarter to take the easiest courses, so I can get good grades.

Reality: Dumb decision. Colleges expect you to take the most challenging courses offered, as long as you can earn decent grades. But if you can't handle the honors course and you're looking at really low grades, then it is better to take courses at the level you can handle. Push yourself, but be realistic.

Myth: I've finished my junior year with good grades and did well on my SAT's. Now I can party, party, party as a senior!

Reality: Wrong, wrong, wrong! Colleges pay close attention to your senior year transcripts for both the fall and spring semesters. If you really goof off, they may actually revoke (yes, cancel!) an acceptance offer. So don't cave now! It's a phenomenon known as senioritis, and it can be deadly.

standardized tests

How important are they?

When people talk about standardized tests, they are usually referring to the **SAT** or **ACT**, college admissions tests. Taking one of these two tests is required by just about every college (see a timeline on page 12). Most accept scores from either test, but some specify one or the other (see pages 116–119) and others may also require SAT II's. A perfect score in the SAT is 800 on the verbal skills and 800 on the math skills, or a total of 1,600. A perfect score on the ACT is 36 for each of the four sections. For the ACT, colleges look mainly at your **composite score**, which is the average of the four sections.

These tests have become a source of anxiety, intense competition, and controversy, none of it good for students or their parents. So really, how important are they? Just about every admissions officer will tell you that the value of test scores is overblown, and that your high school record is more important than SAT (or ACT) results in gaining admission to college. They'll also say that these test scores will never be the sole factor in an admissions decision.

On the other hand, the fact is that for admission to the most sought-after schools with huge numbers of applicants, test scores are very important. At Harvard, for example, combined SAT test scores hover around 1400 and up. Two trends have combined in recent years to pile on the pressure for students to get ever higher scores: the increased competition for the same number of places at selective schools, and the influence of high-profile magazine ranking lists. These lists use SAT scores as a factor in a college's ranking, adding to the pressure colleges are under to choose students with the highest test scores.

The Good News on Test Scores

■ Many colleges, aside from the most highly selective ones, accept students with lower scores than you might think, so don't give up hope if you didn't crack 700, 600, or even 500 on your SAT math or verbal test.

Get a college handbook (see page 20) and flip through to the freshman college profiles for an array of schools. The SAT scores are usually reported as the range in the 50th percentile. Remember, this means that the lowest score is not a cutoff. A quarter of the students in the freshman class scored lower than this range and a quarter scored higher.

For example, the mid 50% range for UCLA in 2002 was 540–650 in verbal and 570–680 in math. So a quarter of the class scored below 540 in verbal and below 570 in math. Let the data help you identify colleges that make sense for you, and don't panic. You'll find some good ones.

■ Most students can improve their scores by prepping. (See page 124.)

■ Some schools don't require the tests. Mount Holyoke, the venerable women's college in Massachusetts, is one of the most prestigious examples of this small but growing trend. See www.fairtest.org to find others.

■ Students with LD's (learning disabilities) or other disabilities can apply for special accommodations when taking these tests. For more information, see page 126.

extracurricular activities

All work and no play

Why do colleges care if you play the triangle in the marching band, warm the bench on the baseball team, or hide in the chorus of the school musical?

Students who have joined clubs, played sports, and held positions in student government show schools the potential to make a significant contribution to campus life. Colleges also view extracurriculars as character building. When you volunteer at your local soup kitchen or get up at 5 A.M. on Saturday to practice soccer with your team, you are demonstrating commitment, dedication, and willingness to sacrifice.

The key word is commitment. Colleges aren't looking for a laundry list of activities. They want evidence of sincere interest and sustained involvement over the high school years. Be able to show how you have made a genuine contribution, but don't overbook yourself.

Keep a balance between academics and extracurricular activities and you'll have a great time in high school and help strengthen your college applications, too.

Common Extracurricular Activities

Clubs Most schools have several clubs, from drama, photography, or chess to a branch of Amnesty International. Don't be shy about joining. Since you'll share a common interest with other club members, you'll soon make friends.

Student government Get involved; you'll learn effective ways to make a difference. Head a committee, then run for president. Why not?

Sports You don't have to be focused on a professional career to play and enjoy sports. Just expect practice times and games to fill up your schedule—and your parents', if they have to drive you to games and drills.

Jobs Successfully holding any job demonstrates maturity and responsibility; try to save some of your earnings for college.

Community service Community service is a great way to do good in an area of interest you won't find in school. See your guidance counselor for suggestions, or contact your local chamber of commerce, United Way, cultural organizations, libraries, or hospitals.

Band If music is your thing, join a school band, orchestra, or chorus, or find somewhere to play or sing in your community.

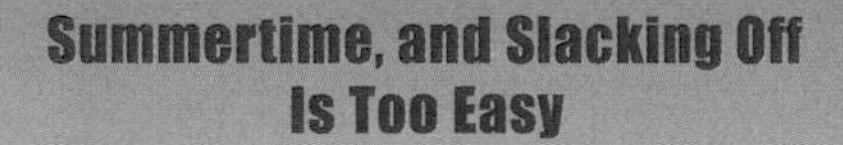

Summertime, and Slacking Off Is Too Easy

Make good use of your summers. It could be as simple as a summer job. Other ideas: volunteering, internships, even college summer programs. Global Routes (**www.globalroutes.org**) offers high school community service programs in countries ranging from Belize to Thailand. Interlocken (**www.interlocken.org**) in New Hampshire, has a Crossroads program that includes adventure travel in Colorado and traveling minstrels in Europe. Outward Bound (**www.outwardbound.com**) offers hundreds of outdoor skills and leadership-building courses. See your guidance counselor for suggestions or check out the myFootpath Web site at **www.myfootpath.com**.

for certified slackers

Making up for lost time

What if you don't look the way admissions officers want you to? What if you don't take **AP** (Advanced Placement) classes, earn top grades, or get good scores on the **SAT** or other college admissions tests? Don't worry. Most people don't earn top grades or high SAT scores—after all, that's what "high" and "top" mean.

Still, you will have to make some adjustments in your expectations and study habits. First of all, if you have good extracurriculars or other interesting activities, you may be able to get into a good school anyway. If not, it's time to strategize.

One common way to fix a shaky high school record is to start at a college that's easier to get into, often a two-year college, then transfer to a four-year school to finish. Community colleges usually offer **open admissions**, which means they accept anyone with a high school diploma. In your first two years, talk to an advisor and make sure you enroll in what's called the transfer program or academic track, which is academic courses that four-year colleges will accept for credit and will prepare you for upper-classmen work.

Wherever you go, work hard and you'll have an excellent shot at being accepted by a much better four-year college than you do right now.

ASK THE EXPERTS

How do I know what two-year colleges to apply to?

Check the two-year college profiles in a good general college guide book or *Peterson's Two-Year Colleges*. Those with a high percentage of transfer students are the ones you want to apply to, because it's an indication of a good academic program with a culture that expects you to move on, and knows how to help you do it.

When should I start thinking about transferring?

It's common to transfer after two years. This way you can establish a much better record. You can try after one year, but if you have a poor high school record, many schools may want to see more evidence that you've really turned yourself around. Speak to the transfer advisor early and often. Even if you transfer after two years, you should have the process in motion by the fall of your sophomore year.

FIRST PERSON SUCCESS STORY

Ugly Duckling Turns Swan

I was so bummed out when it came time to apply to college. I'd fooled around all through high school, and now, just when I started to feel more mature and ready, I had only my lousy high school record to offer college admissions officers. Well, they weren't buying, so I went to the local community college. I hated living with my parents while all my friends went away to school, but I was surprised at how good the community college was. I made sure I was enrolled in the transfer program, and believe me, coming home every day to my same old room was a serious motivator! After two years, I transferred to an excellent four-year college, where I'm living in a dorm, earning top grades, and having the time of my life. Though I never thought I'd say this, those two years at home turned out to be a really good experience. I did need more time to grow up and improve my study habits. Now I'm thinking about graduate school, and this time around my chances of getting into my dream school are pretty good!

—Brian C., Dobbs Ferry, New York

now what do I do?

Answers to common questions

I'm a sophomore and I work at a movie theater as an usher. This doesn't leave much time for school activities, but I like earning the money. How will colleges rank my work experience?

If you have to work to help out at home or to help pay for college, that says a lot about your character, and you'll want to explain that in your application or essay. But also find time to develop a hobby or volunteer in your community, because it will show college admissions folks that you will make a contribution to campus life. Plus doing different things allows you to uncover what skills you have and what you like to do, experiences that will help you pick a career you'd enjoy. Many applicants juggle both work and extracurricular activities. If you discover the right fit, you'll not only help others, have fun, and find personal satisfaction, but also have great practice for the real world!

I didn't take that many AP classes. Should I forget about applying to selective colleges?

You can go ahead and apply to a couple as your outside possibilities, but it will affect how the colleges view your application if the AP's were offered in your school. Some schools, however, don't care as much about the AP's as your grades, and remember, other factors go into your application. Do you have other ways to make yourself attractive to a school? Are you a great athlete or musician? A poet? A political activist? Emphasize these. Another option is to apply to good schools that aren't quite as selective as the very top tier. Applying to a mix of schools is always the best approach.

Should I take the SAT more than once?

Absolutely! Unless you did super well, it's a good idea to try it at least twice, because you will probably raise your score with practice and also with additional coursework under your belt. Take time to prepare for the exams and improve any areas of weakness. For specifics, see chapter 6.

Do lots of kids transfer?

Yes, it's very common. In fact, some statistics say that up to 25% of all college students transfer to a different school. But remember, the quality of your coursework will determine where you can transfer to. Don't put yourself in the same situation twice—do your very best if you want to gain admission to a more prestigious school. Also, keep your expectations within reason. Some of the more selective schools have very few openings for transfers, because they don't lose as many students in the upper grades as the less selective colleges do. And they still will have stricter admissions requirements.

What is the International Baccalaureate?

Offered in a relatively small number of U.S. high schools (just over 400), **International Baccalaureate (IB)** courses can also, at many colleges, result in advanced college credit or standing. This is a very tough series of classes taken in the junior and senior year, with its own set of standardized exams, administered in May. If you pass them all, you earn an IB diploma, which makes you eligible for entrance to international universities where you might otherwise need additional coursework. IB courses were originally developed for the children of diplomats who often move every four years. The courses ensure that wherever they study, there will be a standardized curriculum. Many schools that offer the IB's have a large international population, but the program has become popular domestically as well, because of its quality and rigor.

Now where do I go?

CONTACTS

GoCollege
www.gocollege.com

Global Routes
www.globalroutes.org
High school community service programs in countries ranging from Belize to Thailand.

Outward Bound
www.outwardbound.com
Hundreds of outdoor skills and leadership-building courses.

myFootpath
www.myfootpath.com
College prep program.

www.braintrack.com
Global list of colleges.

www.collegeexpress.com
Tips for parents and students.

PUBLICATIONS

Rugg's Recommendations on the Colleges
By Frederick E. Rugg

The Truth About Getting In: A Top College Advisor Tells You Everything You Need to Know
By Katherine Cohen

The Fiske Guide to Getting into the Right College
By Edward B. Fiske and Bruce G. Hammond

Presenting Yourself Successfully to Colleges: How to Market Your Strengths and Make Your Application Stand Out
By Howard Greene and Matthew W. Greene

chapter 5

How do I go about setting up an interview?
Check out page 103

Applying

the form

The Common Application becomes more common

Each college has its own application form or uses the Common Application. There is basic information to fill out, such as your name and address, along with instructions for how to arrange to send the other information (test scores, essay, recommendations, transcript) that the college requires. You can call and request that an application be mailed to you or, in most cases, download it from the college's Web site. Many colleges now accept the **Common Application,** a generic form that can be sent to multiple colleges. You can access the Common Application at **www.commonapp.org**. At that site you can also see a list of 227 colleges that accept it.

The Common Application is a terrific timesaver. You fill out just one form and send it to all the schools on your list that accept it, rather than filling out lots of different applications. Some schools let you e-mail the form to them, others require you to download it; fill it out by hand, and mail it back. Some colleges that accept the Common Application also require supplemental forms. Check the College Info table at **commonapp.org** for details, or inquire at your prospective college's admissions office.

Applying online

Many colleges will accept your application online. It's a great option, because you can send a much neater application than if you did it by hand. Check the school's guidelines and follow them very carefully, especially any rules about fees and signatures.

FIRST PERSON DISASTER STORY

Make a List and Check It Twice

I was really relieved that I finished all my application stuff before the holidays in December. I just kicked back, relaxed, and went out with my friends. When January rolled around, my mom kept bugging me to call the schools and make sure all my materials were in for my applications, but I'd taken care of everything, so I figured, why worry? Then I happened to be looking at the Web site for my top school and just decided to check in on my status—you know, with some schools you can track your application online. I almost choked—they had never received my transcript! I begged my high school records office to send one in a day. The college said it sent me a "missing item" note, but I never saw that. It all worked out O.K. in the end, but I could have saved myself a whole lot of stress if I'd just checked on this a little sooner.

—Rudy I., Kansas City, Missouri

COMMON APPLICATION® 2002–2003

APPLICATION FOR UNDERGRADUATE ADMISSION

The member colleges and universities listed above encourage the use of this form. No distinction will be made between it and the college's own form. Please type or print in black ink.
Be sure to follow the instructions on the cover page of the Common App booklet to complete, copy, and file your application with any one or several of the member colleges.

PERSONAL DATA

PERSONAL STATEMENT

This personal statement helps us become acquainted with you in ways different from courses, grades, test scores, and other objective data. It will demonstrate your ability to organize thoughts and express yourself. We are looking for an essay that will help us know you better as a person and as a student. Please write an essay (250–500 words) on a topic of your choice or on one of the options listed below. You may attach your essay on separate sheets (same size, please). Also, please indicate your topic by checking the appropriate box below.

☐ 1. Evaluate a significant experience, achievement, risk you have taken, or ethical dilemma you have faced and its impact on you.

☐ 2. Discuss some issue of personal, local, national, or international concern and its importance to you.

☐ 3. Indicate a person who has had a significant influence on you, and describe that influence.

☐ 4. Describe a character in fiction, an historical figure, or a creative work (as in art, music, science, etc.) that has had an influence on you, and explain that influence.

☐ 5. Topic of your choice.

ACADEMIC HONORS

Briefly describe any scholastic distinctions or honors you have won beginning with ninth grade:

EXTRACURRICULAR, PERSONAL, AND VOLUNTEER ACTIVITIES (including summer)

Please list your principal extracurricular, community, and family activities and hobbies in the order of their interest to you. Include specific events and/or major accomplishments such as musical instrument played, varsity letters earned, etc. Check (✓) in the right column those activities you hope to pursue in college. To allow us to focus on the highlights of your activities, please complete this section even if you plan to attach a résumé.

Activity	Grade level or post-secondary (PS)					Approximate time spent		Positions held, honors won, or letters earned	Do you plan to participate in college?
	9	10	11	12	PS	Hours per week	Weeks per year		
	☐	☐	☐	☐	☐				☐
	☐	☐	☐	☐	☐				☐
	☐	☐	☐	☐	☐				☐
	☐	☐	☐	☐	☐				☐

WORK EXPERIENCE

List any job (including summer employment) you have held during the past three years.

Source: The Common Application, www.commonapp.org.

application at a glance

"Apply yourself" never meant so much

It takes a lot of pieces to make up a complete college application. Making sure that all the necessary materials are complete and submitted before the deadline is surely the easiest part of the application process, but you'd be surprised how many students fall behind. Staying organized and taking things step by step will give you an advantage over many other equally qualified, slightly less on-the-ball applicants. And every little bit counts! For information about admissions requirements, you can't beat the colleges' own Web sites, which are much more extensive and easily accessible than their printed literature. Many colleges even let you track the status of your application online, including letting you know which forms they have not received.

Step by Step

Filling Out the Application

1. Download the application off the college's Web site, or call to get one mailed to you. More and more colleges take applications online—you fill them out at the college Web site—but you should download the old-fashioned version first anyway so you can plan carefully before forging ahead.

2. Read through the application carefully, noting deadlines, essay topics, and specific requirements. (For instance, do they want SAT II scores?) Follow all directions carefully.

3. Make a copy! Don't put pen to paper until you have a copy to work with. Fill it out for practice so you don't make any dopey mistakes, like putting your father's name in the box for your mother's.

4. When you've filled out your duplicate form, have somebody you trust (someone with good proofreading skills) look it over.

5. If it's all O.K., copy everything onto a clean application form. Use blue or black ink—or if you have access to a typewriter and have good lining-up skills, type it. If you're applying online, carefully type in each field in the Web site's application form.

6. Work very carefully! If you're writing by hand, neatness counts. And whether you're writing or typing, check you don't make mistakes. If you mess up on paper, print out another copy and start again—or if the mistake's tiny, white it out neatly.

7. Have someone proofread the final copy. (Sound obsessive? Hey, there's a lot at stake here! If you send in a mistake-free application, it'll put you ahead of equally qualified students who don't take the time.)

8. Get to work on your essay (see page 98).

9. Arrange to have all other information (transcripts, test scores, recommendations) sent. Stay on top of this, and check again as deadlines near. You may have to issue polite reminders.

10. Make a photocopy of your completed application for your files. Never omit this step! If it is lost, you'll have to submit a new application.

11. Attach your check to the original application. Sign your application.

12. Give the application, check, and essay to your guidance counselor, if that's the procedure at your school, or if there's any part that the guidance counselor needs to fill out. Otherwise, take it to the post office and make sure you have the correct postage. Do not use overnight delivery because it shows you are deadline aversive.

13. Follow up with a phone call in about a week, to make sure the college received the application. If you applied online, check your e-mail or log in to the college's site to see how your application's proceeding.

14. As deadlines near, call the colleges to make sure they've received everything (transcripts, recommendations, etc.). Don't assume it's all O.K.—be certain.

Here's a Checklist of What Most Colleges Want.

Application form
Transcript
Test scores
Your essay
Recommendations
Visit and Interview
Portfolios or auditions
Application fee

sending your transcript

Special handling

The single most important document for applying to college is your transcript, or high school record, which shows all your courses and grades from freshman year through whatever point you've reached in your senior year.

Your transcript tells colleges whether or not

- You've met their basic course requirements.
- You've challenged yourself academically.
- You've done well in your course work, or show the potential to do well.

In order to avoid tampering, your transcript must be sent directly to the colleges on your list by your school records office, not by you. Colleges may require the envelope containing your transcript to be sealed and signed across the flap. See each individual school's rules and exceptions.

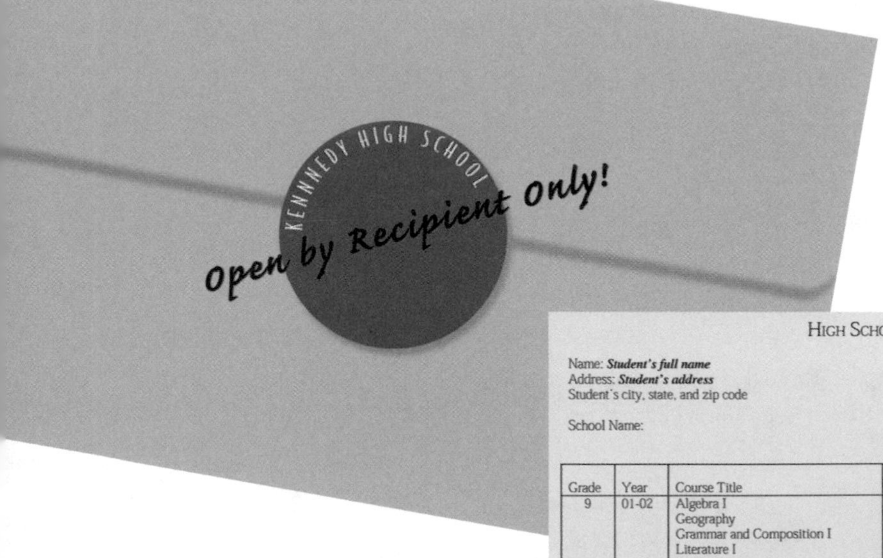

KENNEDY HIGH SCHOOL

Open by Recipient Only!

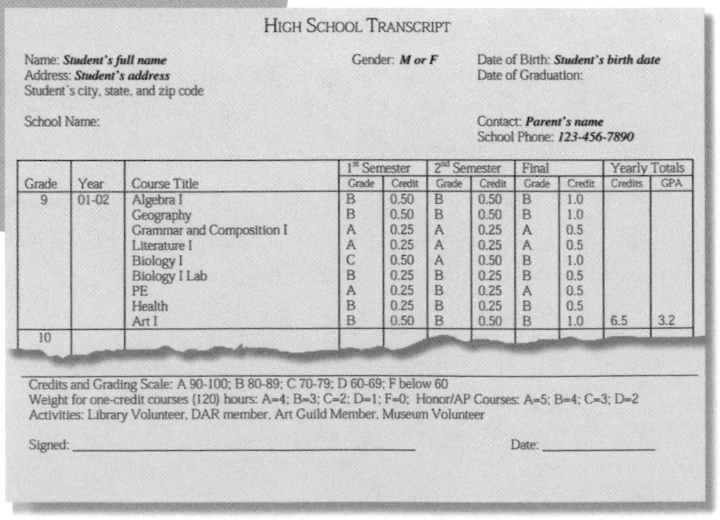

HIGH SCHOOL TRANSCRIPT

Name: ***Student's full name***
Address: ***Student's address***
Student's city, state, and zip code

Gender: ***M or F***

Date of Birth: ***Student's birth date***
Date of Graduation:

School Name:

Contact: ***Parent's name***
School Phone: ***123-456-7890***

Grade	Year	Course Title	1st Semester		2nd Semester		Final		Yearly Totals	
			Grade	Credit	Grade	Credit	Grade	Credit	Credits	GPA
9	01-02	Algebra I	B	0.50	B	0.50	B	1.0		
		Geography	B	0.50	B	0.50	B	1.0		
		Grammar and Composition I	A	0.25	A	0.25	A	0.5		
		Literature I	A	0.25	A	0.25	A	0.5		
		Biology I	C	0.50	A	0.50	B	1.0		
		Biology I Lab	B	0.25	B	0.25	B	0.5		
		PE	A	0.25	B	0.25	A	0.5		
		Health	B	0.25	B	0.25	B	0.5		
		Art I	B	0.50	B	0.50	B	1.0	6.5	3.2
10										

Credits and Grading Scale: A 90-100; B 80-89; C 70-79; D 60-69; F below 60
Weight for one-credit courses (120) hours: A=4; B=3; C=2; D=1; F=0; Honor/AP Courses: A=5; B=4; C=3; D=2
Activities: Library Volunteer, DAR member, Art Guild Member, Museum Volunteer

Signed: ______________________ Date: ____________

ASK THE EXPERTS

How do I have my transcript sent?

Some college applications come with a transcript form that you take to your school records office or your guidance counselor. Even if there is no special form with the application, there will be instructions telling you that you need to have your grades sent. School records offices usually have a transcript request form for each college you are applying to. You fill out the request form, then they take care of sending your transcript.

How do I know that my transcript is accurate?

Ask for a copy of your transcript and read it carefully. It's not secret—this isn't the mythical "permanent record" that contains your worst exploits from third grade—so you shouldn't have a problem obtaining one. Make sure all your grades are accurate, and that the A you got in creative writing last year didn't somehow go missing. File this copy away carefully at home.

My school gave me an envelope with a copy of my transcript and told me to send it. Can I look inside?

Though most school's records offices will send transcripts directly to colleges, at some schools the procedure is different. If they give it to you in a sealed envelope, you must leave it sealed and attach it to your application. As cloak-and-dagger as it sounds, don't look in that envelope. Just restrain your curiosity and stick it in the mail. If you open it, it's no longer official (you could have tampered with it) and the college might not accept it.

One college I applied to wants to see reports from later in my senior year. How do I make that happen?

If the colleges require midyear reports, ask your guidance counselor or school records office how to have that done. Sometimes the office automatically sends your midyear and even end-of-year transcripts to all the colleges you have applied to.

test results

Getting your scores sent

Most college applications require you to send them the results of your standardized test scores. To find out what admissions tests a college requires, check the college's application form. You can also consult the school's profile in your college guidebook. Your best bet is to check the admissions requirements online on the college's Web site or call the admissions office.

Usually, at a minimum, you must take either the SAT or the ACT. (See all about tests on pages 80–81.) Most colleges accept the scores from either test, but some require one or the other. Some of the more selective colleges also have you take three or more SAT II's, which are achievement tests in various subjects. The SAT II writing test is often required.

If you are taking any other college-related tests, such as those for college credit (see the AP, the IB, and the CLEP, page 122), you should also have those scores sent to the colleges on your list. With so many initials, these tests can start to look like alphabet soup. To find out what they mean, see chapter 6.

TEST INFORMATION

Be sure to note the tests required for each institution to which you are applying. The official scores from the appropriate testing agency must be submitted to each institution as soon as possible. Please list your test plans below.

ACT	Date Taken/ To Be Taken	English Score	Math Score	Reading Score	Science Score	Composite Score			
	Date Taken	English Score	Math Score	Reading Score	Science Score	Composite Score			
SAT I	Date Taken/ To Be Taken	Verbal Score	Math Score	Date	Verbal Score	Math Score			
SAT II Subject Tests	Date	Subject	Score	Date	Subject	Score	Date	Subject	Score
	Date	Subject	Score	Date	Subject	Score	Date	Subject	Score
Test of English as a second language (TOEFL or other exam)	Test	Date Taken/ To Be Taken	Score	Test	Date Taken/ To Be Taken	Score			

Source: The Common Application, www.commonapp.org.

ASK THE EXPERTS

When should I take the tests?

You should definitely take the SAT or the ACT near the end of your junior year. This gives you time to take it again in the fall of your senior year if you need to improve your scores. Also, if you decide to apply on an early-decision basis, you may not get your scores in on time if you wait to take the exams in the fall. Keep in mind that you have to register several weeks in advance to take the tests. It's also a good idea to take the SAT II's and any AP's at the end of each year, just when you've finished the course material for those subjects. It's much easier than reviewing a year later!

How do I register for college admissions tests?

Your guidance counselor will have registration packets that you can fill out by hand and mail in, along with a fee, or for the SAT and the ACT you can register online (which is much faster for the SAT). For complete information on registering for the SAT, SAT II, AP or CLEP, go to **www.collegeboard.com**; for the ACT, go to **www.act.org**. The instructions are very clear, and you'll find test dates and deadlines for the entire year.

Your admission ticket should arrive in the mail well in advance of the test date. Check that all the information on it is correct, then take it with you on the day of the test, along with the other materials it specifies you should bring: acceptable ID, two no. 2 pencils, and, if allowed, a calculator. Show up early, because if you're late they won't let you in.

writing the essay

Smart, personal, and spelled correctly

Excuses, Excuses

If some aspect of your high school record needs explaining (illness, leave of absence, a disastrous semester), some experts suggest that you attach a short personal statement to your application, in addition to your essay. Avoid the sob story, and don't ramble. Explain clearly and keep it positive.

A lot of the factors that go into your college application are statistics: your grades, class standing, SAT scores, and so forth. By the time you get around to filling out the college applications, there may not be much you can do to change these. But the essay is one area where you can take charge and make a difference. Most colleges ask you to write an essay as part of the application for admission. They may ask you to answer a question or offer you a choice of questions on different topics to answer in essay form.

This is where the real you steps off the page and greets the admissions committee. While giving them a better picture of the sort of person you are, it also indicates how well you write, spell, proofread your work, and pay attention to detail. A good essay also shows clear, logical thinking. Your essay is not going to override a poor academic record, but it may, in a borderline instance, tip the balance in your favor. (And a messy, badly written, poorly proofread one can tilt the balance in the opposite direction.) So it's well worth your while to write the most honest, original, and interesting essay you can. Be sure to answer the question that is asked.

Essay tips

There is so much advice out there these days about writing the college essay (entire books!)—and so much exaggeration—that you may feel you have to be a Tolstoy or wither under the scorn of the admissions committee. But take heart. Your essay doesn't have to be a work of towering genius, and admissions officers are not literary critics. Follow these tips, and the words should start to flow.

- **Know your topic** Some colleges give you a choice, but others leave it up to you. Whatever you choose, make sure it's something you know and care about, and that you do actually write about the topic you choose.
- **Outline your ideas** There should be a logical flow.

■ **Try to think of an original way to put your points across** But don't try too hard to be cute or you may turn off your readers. Sounds unfair, doesn't it? How do you know the difference? Talk your topic over with someone with good writing skills: an English teacher, a parent, a friend, whoever. They may help you come up with an interesting approach.

■ **Be upbeat!** It's positive energy, not negative, that makes people respond favorably to you. Colleges want to know how you've resolved difficulties, not how you are laboring under them. They want to know you have what it takes to succeed—they don't want to hear a long, whining story about how unfair life is.

■ **Avoid clichés** An essay on a unique or personal topic will stand out.

■ **Write honestly and from the heart** This is where you will find your voice. Don't try to sound like someone else you think the college might like better. That rarely works.

■ **Be sure to answer the question that's asked!**

■ **Show your essay** to at least a couple of people you trust—your English teacher or guidance counselor, for example. Don't be insulted if they give you a lot of suggestions—be grateful. Even the best writers benefit from good editing.

■ **Write your essay in advance** so you have time to proofread it carefully, and ask other people to proofread it, too. No grammatical errors, no misspellings.

You can also find essays and critiques at **www.collegeboard.com**, click getting into college, and essay writing tips. See samples of essays that worked at **www.conncoll.edu/admissions/essays/index.html**.

recommendations

What people say about you

Most colleges ask for at least one or two recommendations from teachers or other adults who know you well. Sometimes the application packet includes a recommendation form, but sometimes you just ask someone to write a letter.

Think carefully about the right people to ask for recommendations. Recommendations, along with your essay, are the most personally revealing parts of the application. You want someone who is genuinely enthusiastic about you to write yours. Also, you don't want to put a teacher on the spot if he or she has some hesitation about your abilities.

Don't expect a teacher to write a different version of a recommendation for you for each school. Commonly, the teacher writes one recommendation, prints out several copies, and signs one for each school. Your most recent teachers are the ones who are the most credible to the admissions committee.

Step by Step

Securing a Recommendation

1. Once you know which colleges you are applying to, figure out how many recommendations you need.

2. Decide which teachers you will ask. Assume you will send their same recommendations to each school.

3. Approach those teachers early in the fall, so you give them plenty of time, and ask if they would be willing to write references for you.

4. If they agree, give them stamped, addressed envelopes for each college you want their recommendations sent to; do this promptly after getting their permission. If a college uses a form, provide this too.

5. Sometimes busy teachers need help. Ask if they would like a copy of your résumé or any other information that would be useful. For example, if you tell them you hope to be a music major, they can address your talents in that area more specifically.

6. Don't ask to see what they write. Sign the waiver on the form (provided with your college application kit) agreeing that you will not see the completed form. This increases the recommendation's credibility.

7. About a month after giving the recommenders the envelopes (or if you are nearing the application deadline), check with the colleges to make sure they've received the recommendations. If not, go back to your teachers with a gentle reminder. At some schools, the records office coordinates the sending of recommendations and will follow up with the teachers. Ask your guidance counselor how it works at your school, and always be tactful. Most teachers are very conscientious, but they can get buried in paperwork.

8. Once the recommendations have been received at the colleges, follow up with a thank-you note to each teacher.

the interview

What to say, what to ask

Although many colleges these days say interviews are optional and only for informational purposes, most of the better schools still "recommend" them if possible, and a few still require them (these are known as "evaluative" interviews, and they are a definite part of the admissions process). Go for an interview at any college to which you are applying—if they accept interviews.

Here's why: Even at the schools where interviews are said to be simply **informational** (for you to have your questions answered), you will be meeting with an admissions officer and getting a shot at leaving a good impression. This is an opportunity for you to make a personal connection, show a genuine interest, and otherwise stand out from the crowd. Use every chance you can to increase your advantage. Having a personal connection may tip the scales in your favor. What's more, you can really get a much better feel for the place, and discuss your academic plans with the admissions counselor. So go very well prepared (read all the available materials ahead of time) and have your questions ready. (For more advice on interviewing, see the campus visit, page 44.)

Some of the colleges that require an interview may not be able to handle the volume of applicants, so you may actually be interviewed by a graduate of the college, and the interview may be held with a resident in the area, rather than on campus. (When you realize that some schools, like Harvard, get nearly 20,000 applicants, it's obvious that the admissions staff can't see everyone.) For these interviews, you should definitely prepare and practice ahead of time with your parents. Also, be ready to speak about yourself. Take a résumé and have something to say about subjects that interest you, what your academic goals are, and why you are interested in this particular school.

One Web site you can try for more interviewing tips is **www.collegeapps.about.com/cs/interview**, where they have a link to interviewing tips from the admissions staff at Union College.

ASK THE EXPERTS

How do I go about setting up an interview?

Call well in advance to make sure the college accepts interviews. Most colleges offer interviews (usually a half-hour) daily, and group tours (45 minutes to an hour) several times each day. You may also want to meet other people, like a coach or financial aid officer, or arrange an overnight stay. Tell the admissions officer what you'd like and he or she will advise you on how to set up other meetings.

What should I wear?

Dress conservatively. Nothing too formal, but definitely not casual. Put on what you would normally wear when going to a special function with adults. You don't have to wear a suit, but nix the jeans and sneakers—neat, semidressy clothes are just right.

What should I do once I arrive there?

First, arrive on time. Leave your parents in the waiting room. This is about you. Be pleasant and positive, make eye contact, sit up, and speak up. And finally, be prepared. Bring a copy of your transcript. Read all the literature before you go, so you can ask intelligent, informed questions. Leave time to ask questions that pertain specifically to you—your academic and career goals, or your athletic or extracurricular plans, for example. Be ready to discuss the things you say interest you. Have a list of questions ready.

What do I do when the interview is over?

Shake hands, smile, and thank the admissions officer. Get his or her card, and follow up with a thank-you note.

portfolios and auditions

Showcasing your talent

If you are applying to an art school, or an art program at a liberal arts college, you will usually have to present evidence of your talent in addition to the regular application.

If you're a budding Picasso, you will probably be asked to submit a portfolio of samples of your work. If you are applying to a performing arts program (music, dance, theater) you will almost always have to audition. Film schools vary in their requirements.

Read all the admissions materials carefully early on to find out what extra requirements you must fulfill. They are very detailed, and you need to follow instructions exactly. Don't delay. Portfolios take time to prepare, and audition appointments can fill up quickly.

Typical Portfolio and Audition Requirements

Fine arts majors will be asked to send in samples of their work. The required format will vary, from sketch pads to portfolios of slides of your work. The instructions are usually very specific concerning the number of pieces or slides you submit, their size, labeling requirements, range of content, and so forth.

Dance students typically are required to submit a résumé, photo, and recommendations, and to audition. Again, requirements vary but are quite specific. You may be required to bring a cassette of music, of an exact duration, perform certain types of pieces, and participate in a class. You may also be interviewed.

Musicians will almost certainly have to audition. You will probably have to indicate your area of interest (jazz, voice, instrumental, studio production or composition, etc.), and in addition you may be requested to bring samples of your performances on tape or CD.

Theater schools or acting academies also require auditions. Again, you will find very specific instructions on the Web site or in the admissions materials on how to schedule the audition and prepare for it, including the types of pieces required, the length of each, what to wear, and what to bring (usually a résumé and a head shot). The audition time is generally quite short—just a few minutes in total. Some schools, like the State University of New York at Purchase, hold auditions in several major cities around the country.

Film schools vary in their requirements quite a bit. Some schools grant interviews and accept samples of any film or scriptwriting you've done, but others, like the School of Cinema-Television at USC, do not give interviews. Instead, they require several supplemental forms with the application, including a personal statement about why you want to study film, a portfolio list of creative work (not necessarily film), extra writing samples, and several letters of recommendation.

transfers

Second chances

College students transfer for many reasons. Some go to junior colleges and therefore have to transfer to a four-year school if they want to earn a B.A. Others, with spotty high school records, begin at a less selective school and after a year or two of better grades want to try gaining admittance to a more selective school. Still others find that for whatever reason—academic, financial, or personal—the school that seemed right at the end of their high school years just doesn't fit after all.

While it's common to transfer at the end of sophomore year, you can transfer after one year or even midyear. It depends on the circumstances and requirements of the college you are considering. If you think when you start as a freshman that you may want to transfer, see an academic advisor and make sure you are taking courses that will be acceptable for credit at other institutions.

As far as finding schools to transfer to, you will have to assess why you are transferring. Are you in a rural area and find that you hate cows? Did you start out as a dance major, and now you want to be a neurosurgeon? If so, go back on the Web, speak to an advisor, and do the research all over again. When you call the admissions offices, ask to speak to a transfer counselor.

The Transfer's Application Package

Transfer applicants will have to follow many of the same steps as in applying to college the first time around. Generally, you will have to submit:

- **An application.** Some colleges have a specific transfer application. Others, like Harvard, accept the Common Application with a transfer application supplement. This will include the essay.

- **An official college transcript.** This is the most important document. Colleges are trying to predict how well you will perform college-level work. Here's the proof. But remember, colleges will still be looking not only at grades, but at the level of difficulty of the courses you take.

- **An official high school transcript.** Yes, good or bad, they'll want to see it. But if you've gone from C's and D's in high school to A's in college, that will help tremendously.

- **SAT or ACT scores.** These scores may be required. If they were low, you may want to try again. No need to submit SAT II's.

- At least one **recommendation** from a college professor.

- **Catalog descriptions,** plus detailed course descriptions handed out by the department or professor of courses you've taken, to help the college determine how much credit they will give you.

- **Financial aid application.** Most schools award financial aid to transfer students. It's basically the same process to apply for this aid as for regular aid, but you can't expect exactly the same amount of aid as at your current school. Speak to the financial aid officer so you know what to expect, fill out the forms, and see what sort of package you might be able to receive.

Housing For Transfer Students

Some colleges guarantee housing only for freshmen, so don't forget to ask about housing when you speak with the transfer counselor. You'll be entering a new community as an upperclassman, and if you can't get into a dorm, it will be much harder to make new friends.

now what do I do?

Answers to common questions

Does it help to tell a college it's my number one choice? (Some of my applications asked that question.)

If you truly have your sights set on one school, definitely tell them. It may swing a decision in your favor. While of course colleges want to keep their overall averages (SAT, GPA, etc.) high, they also want to find students who will say "yes." That's because magazines and other sources that rank colleges often take a look at the number of accepted students who choose to enroll (in other words, what percentage of students, out of the total number accepted, actually enrolled). This percentage is known as the "**yield.**" If they know you're a sure thing, that may work to your advantage.

Should I attach any other materials to my application?

Although most colleges don't ask for a résumé, it's a good idea to include one. Most applications don't leave enough room for all your extracurricular activities, jobs, and awards, so you might have to attach a separate page anyway. Preparing a résumé has another benefit—it helps you clarify what your achievements are and put them all down clearly in one place. You may be surprised at how much you've accomplished. This can be a big help in speaking positively (but not boastfully) about yourself during interviews.

What about writing samples?

Some applications also invite you to include writing samples, poetry, or other creative work. Don't send everything. Pick a couple of your best works, make good copies, and send them along. If you find there are a lot of pieces to your application package, you may want to put them all in a clear plastic binder. It's neater and shows you care how you present yourself.

Is it a good idea to send lots of extra materials with my application to impress the admissions officers? I want extra credit!

No. Admissions officers are very busy, and they won't appreciate being deluged with materials. They also may not have time to watch a 30-minute personal video you decide to create. Follow their guidelines. Call the admissions office to ask for approval before sending something special you have in mind. If the application says you can send two or three pieces, send two or three pieces. If you send in 20 poems they will only take time to look at a couple, so your best work may never be read. Also, don't send your only copies. The busy admissions staff can't send them back.

How do I transfer credits?

Most schools accept some transfer students. (Be warned, however, that at selective schools the number of transfer students accepted can be very limited.) However, you will find it easier to transfer to colleges that have articulation agreements (carefully worked out transfer credit arrangements) with your current school. Otherwise you will have to negotiate how much credit will be transferable to your new school, and you may not get it all.

Now where do I go?

CONTACTS

www.collegeapps.about.com/cs/interview
Interviewing tips.

www.collegeboard.com
Click on Getting into College and Essay Writing Tips.

PUBLICATIONS

Greenes' Guide to Educational Planning: Presenting Yourself Successfully to Colleges
By Howard Greene and Matthew W. Greene

The Truth About Getting In: A Top College Advisor Tells You Everything You Need to Know
By Katherine Cohen, Ph.D.

The Fiske Guide to Getting into the Right College
By Edward B. Fiske and Bruce G. Hammond

Arco: The Unofficial Guide to College Admissions
By Shannon Turlington

chapter 6

How do I know which tests I need to take?
Check out page 113

The standardized tests

college tests

Let's review

Standardized tests are an unavoidable part of the U.S. educational system, from grade school right on up through college. Almost everyone knows about the SAT, the most common test for college, but there are others too. (See page 12 for a timeline.)

Practice Tests to Help You Prepare
These scores are not reported to colleges.

- The **PSAT/NMSQT** (the Preliminary SAT/National Merit Scholarship Qualifying Test), the practice test for the SAT. Take it in the fall of your junior year. You can also take it in your sophomore year.

- **PLAN**, the practice test for ACT, which some schools offer in tenth grade.

Required Admissions Tests
Almost all colleges require either

- The **SAT**, a three-hour reasoning test on English, math, and writing.

Or

- The **ACT**, a three-hour achievement test on English, reading comprehension, math, and science reasoning.

Some selective schools also require:

- The **SAT II**, subject tests—often two or three of them.

Optional Tests
These tests are for advanced college credit or placement.

- **AP** (Advanced Placement) exams given at the end of the year for AP courses, such as English, that your high school may offer.

- **IB** (International Baccalaureate) exams follow a course of study for an IB diploma or are given after individual IB courses. The program is offered only in about 400 U.S. high schools.

- **CLEP**'s (College-Level Examination Program exams) are tests taken to earn college credit for study done outside of high school, if, for example, you have taken community college courses.

ASK THE EXPERTS

How do I know which tests I need to take?

The profiles in your college guidebook should explain clearly which tests each college requires for admission, and also whether the college accepts Advanced Placement or similar college credit test results. The same information is given on the application and the college's Web site. If you still have questions, call and ask.

How do I go about taking the tests?

It varies. You need to read up on specific information for each test. Some are given several times each year, but the PSAT, for example, is offered only in the fall, and the AP's and IB's are given just in the spring. Ask your guidance counselor.

Where are the tests given?

Locations vary. Some are offered in designated testing centers, some in your school, and some (CLEP) are on college campuses.

Is there a fee to take the tests?

Yes. The fees vary, from $9.50 for the PSAT to a whopping $77 for each AP test. In most cases it's possible to secure a reduced fee or waiver, so if fees pose a financial hardship for you, see your guidance counselor for help.

Where can I find more information about the tests?

For taking the PSAT/NMSQT, SAT, SAT II's, AP's, and CLEP's you will find detailed instructions at **www.collegeboard.com**. For the ACT or PLAN, go to **www.act.org**. For the IB's, which are handled through the school, see your guidance counselor.

To Everything a Season

School admissions testing and other college details undergo reevaluation and change often. See your guidance counselor and the college's Web sites or admissions officers for current information.

practice tests

All about the PSAT/ NMSQT and PLAN

The PSAT/NMSQT and PLAN are both practice exams. They help you assess your strengths and weaknesses and prepare for the SAT and ACT tests you'll take later.

The **PSAT/NMSQT** (Preliminary SAT/National Merit Scholarship Qualifying Test) is taken during your junior year of high school to prepare for taking the SAT. **PLAN**, developed by the same folks who bring you the ACT, is administered in some high schools in the 10th grade. It's up to your high school whether it's offered, so check with your guidance counselor. PLAN can help you choose a major and a career by identifying your interests and skills.

With either exam, don't be discouraged if you don't score as high as you'd like. Remember, this is a practice test. Use the results to determine where you need to study harder before taking the SAT or ACT. Also, keep in mind that scores generally improve the more practice tests you take.

Test Yourself

Here's a sample from the October 1996 PSAT/NMSQT.
If your garden plot is small, it will not pay to grow crops that require a large amount of ---- in order to develop.
(A) sun
(B) rain
(C) fertilizer
(D) space
(E) care
Explanation: In this sentence the key words are "If" and "small." "If" the garden is "small," then the crops will not have a lot of room in which to grow. The answer must be a word that suggests area. Only the word "space," choice (D), does this. Correct Answer: D.

How did you do? See more practice tests at **www.collegeboard.com/testing**.

Source: www.collegeboard.com.

Fast facts: The PSAT/NMSQT

1. The PSAT/NMSQT is a practice exam for the SAT.

2. Most students take the PSAT/NMSQT in the fall of their junior year, when the test also determines candidates for National Merit Scholarships. But some schools offer it to sophomores, so that you can get more practice. Take it as often as you can.

3. Test scores are not reported to colleges.

4. Scoring: Each section is scored from 20 to 80. (If you add a zero, you get an idea of the SAT range, which is scored from 200 to 800 each in math and verbal skill sections.)

5. To register: See your guidance counselor and pick up a copy of the PSAT/NMSQT *Student Bulletin*. You must register through your high school.

6. The test: Five sections, two 25-minute verbal, two 25-minute math, and one 30-minute writing. Total time is two hours, 10 minutes.

Plan

1. PLAN is a practice test for the ACT.
2. PLAN is given in some high schools in the sophomore year. Ask your guidance counselor if your school participates. You cannot register online.
3. Test scores are not reported to colleges.
4. The test: Four sections, one 30-minute English, one 40-minute math, one 20-minute reading, and one 25-minute science reasoning. Total time is one hour, 55 minutes.

How to Prepare

The PSAT/NMSQT *Student Bulletin* has a full-length practice exam you can take. SparkNotes, Princeton, Kaplan are among the publishers that sell books with sample PSAT exams and test-taking strategies. You can also go to the College Board's Web site, where you'll find sample questions, answers, and test-taking tips. Should you wish to prep for PLAN, use any of the ACT prep materials. See pages 119, 124, and 129.

SAT

Bring #2 pencils

The SAT is the most commonly accepted and best known—not to mention infamous—college admissions test. It or the ACT is required by most colleges, and you've probably heard plenty about it by now. Chances are your older siblings or upperclassmates have sweated it and dreaded it, and now it's your turn!

In a nutshell, the SAT is a three-hour, almost entirely multiple-choice exam (there is a very short grid-in section in math). The College Board describes it as a test of your reasoning ability, based upon what you've learned in school. (See box at left for the origin of the SAT name.) It's offered seven times a year, very early (be ready to roll at 8 A.M.!) on Saturday mornings at various testing centers and schools. You can take the test as many times as you want, but each time you have new scores sent to colleges the results of all your tests are sent.

So, is the SAT really as bad as it's made out to be? That depends on how much anxiety you bring to the table. You should definitely prepare for it, take it seriously, and work hard to do well on it. After that, let it go. Concentrate instead on your classes and choosing the schools you want to attend.

Major changes are coming to the SAT in March 2005. Check with your high school guidance counselor for how they may affect you.

The Origin of the SAT

What exactly is the SAT? Critics say that "The Big Test" is little more than an IQ test. Others say that its questions favor white or upper-middle-class students. Its initials used to stand for Scholastic Aptitude Test, then Scholastic Assessment Test, but with the dispute about what it actually measures, it's now just known and pronounced as SAT (rhymes with hat) or by its individual initials S-A-T. The SAT was developed by the Educational Testing Service (ETS), a nonprofit company that develops standardized tests for the College Board, a nonprofit organization of colleges and other educational institutions that administers the SAT's, AP's, and CLEP's.

Fast Facts: The SAT

1. The SAT is the most commonly required college admissions test. Chances are you'll need to take it, unless you apply to the few colleges that do not require it—several hundred out of almost 4,000.

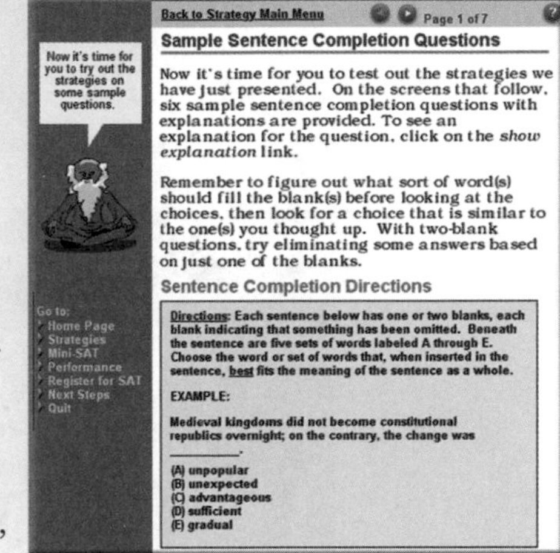

2. The SAT is given seven times each year at selected testing centers. Students usually take it in the spring of their junior year and sometimes again in the fall of their senior year.

3. Test scores: You'll need them for most colleges. You'll get two scores, a verbal and a math. Both range from 200 to 800. Highest possible combined score: 1,600. Average combined score: 1,000.

4. Sending scores to your colleges: When you register to take the test, you can arrange to have your scores sent to four colleges free and, for a fee, to additional colleges, then or later. If you take the test twice, both sets of scores will be sent to the colleges. All sorts of score-reporting services are offered, from analyzing your scores to rushing them, so prices vary. For your options, see **www.collegeboard.com**.

5. The test: Seven sections in total. Three verbal: two 30-minute sections and one 15-minute part. Three math: two 30-minute sections and one 15-minute part. One experimental: a 30-minute section known as the "equating" section. It could be either verbal or math. It won't count toward your score. You won't know which section is experimental—it's the test maker's method to develop new questions for future exams. Total time: Three hours, plus breaks and exam instructions.

6. To register by mail, ask your guidance counselor for the SAT *Registration Bulletin*. Online, go to **www.collegeboard.com**, click on "taking the tests," and follow instructions (it's much easier and faster than by mail). You have to register weeks in advance. Check the deadline.

How to Prepare

First, work hard in your classes and read a lot. But beyond that, most students can improve their scores by prepping. Different ways to prep include practice exams, online tutorials, test-prep books, group classes, or private tutors. See pages 124 and 129.

ACT

Another option instead of the SAT

Although not as well known as the SAT, the ACT is the other commonly accepted college admissions test. It is a multiple-choice exam and takes just under three hours, not including time for breaks. Originally the American College Testing program, it's now known as the plain old A-C-T.

The ACT is offered nationally five times, and in selected states a sixth time, each year. It's also for early risers—you'll have to be there, pencils sharpened, at 8 A.M. on a Saturday morning. Unlike the SAT, the ACT is a **content-based exam**, tied more closely to what you've learned in high school. (The SAT describes itself as a reasoning test.)

One nice thing about the ACT, as opposed to the SAT, is that if you take the exam more than once, you don't have to have cumulative reports of all your scores sent to your colleges. You can choose to send just the scores for the exam you did best on.

Fast Facts: The ACT

1. The ACT (along with the SAT) is the most commonly required college admissions test. Unless you take the SAT or apply only to colleges that do not require either one (a few hundred out of almost 4,000), you will almost certainly have to take it.

2. The ACT is given five times nationally, and a sixth time in selected states, each year. Students often take it in the spring of their junior year, then sometimes again in the fall of their senior year.

3. Test scores: You'll need them for most colleges, unless you take the SAT. You receive separate scores for each of the four sections of the ACT, ranging from 1 to 36 points. You will also get an average, or composite, score (the national being about 21), which is what you see in the college profiles.

4. Sending scores to your colleges: When you register to take the test, you can arrange to have your scores sent to four colleges free and, for a fee, sent to more colleges, then or later. If you take the test more than once, you can choose which scores to send. See **www.act.org**.

5. The test: Four sections in total: English: 45 minutes. Math: 60 minutes. Reading: 35 minutes. Science Reasoning: 35 minutes. Total test time: Two hours 55 minutes, plus breaks and exam instructions.

6. To register by mail, ask your guidance counselor for registration materials. Online, go to **www.act.org**. Unlike the SAT, registering for the ACT online is not much faster than on paper, because they require you to fill out all sorts of extra information.

How to Prepare

As with the SAT, there are test prep books (ask your guidance counselor for the free booklet "Preparing for the ACT Assessment"), online tutorials, private tutors, etc. As with the SAT, scores tend to rise the more you take practice tests. See pages 124 and 129.

SAT II

English, history, math

SAT II exams come as a shock to some students, who think that once the SAT is out of the way all that nasty testing is finished. In fact, some selective colleges also require two or three **SAT II** tests. These commonly include the SAT II writing test plus two others. Some colleges require the math test, others a language exam. Still others leave the choice up to you.

These are one-hour, mostly multiple-choice subject exams, currently offered in five major subject areas: English, History, Math, Science, and Languages. There are 22 different SAT II tests in all.

FIRST PERSON SUCCESS STORY

Practice Makes—Better!

I did very little studying for the PSAT, and when I got my scores back I was totally freaked—they were way lower than I had expected. I started wondering if I would bomb the SAT. But my parents weren't buying that at all and suggested that maybe a little more work preparing would be the answer. It sounded crazy, but they didn't give me any choice, so I enrolled in a test-prep course and found out all sorts of test-taking tips—the most important being that the more you take practice tests, the better you do. In this course, we took a practice SAT (actual tests from previous years—you can get books with these at your bookstore) every other Saturday, and by the time the SAT rolled around in the spring, I felt more relaxed and ready. Best of all, I raised my scores up to the level I had expected in the first place. Practice, practice, practice—it really does pay off.

—Maria C., Phoenix, Arizona

Fast Facts: The SAT II

1. The SAT II exams are one-hour subject tests based upon high school course content. Mostly multiple choice, they are required by some colleges but not by others.

2. SAT IIs are given on six test dates each year, the same dates as for the SAT (except that none are given in March or April). However, you cannot take SAT and SAT IIs on the same day. You can take up to three SAT II exams in one day, but it is not advisable to take more than two (you'll fry your brain) at one sitting. Not every SAT II exam is offered on every test date, so check the schedule at **www.collegeboard.com** (click on "taking the tests," then on SAT II).

3. Test scores: You'll need them for some (usually more selective) colleges. Usually two or three exams, including the SAT II writing tests, are required. You'll get one score, ranging from 200 to 800, for each exam.

4. Sending scores to your colleges: You can arrange to send scores to four colleges free when you register, then add more for a fee, then or later.

5. The test: Each exam is one hour, mostly multiple choice.

6. To register by mail, ask your guidance counselor for a registration packet. Online, go to **www.collegeboard.com**; click on "taking the tests," then on SAT II.

How to Prepare

There are test-prep books at your bookstore, online tutorials, and more. The College Board Web site (**www.collegeboard.com**) has a wealth of information about the SAT II's, including an SAT II Prep Center. You'll find detailed descriptions of each exam's content and format, a calendar giving dates for each test, average national scores for each test, registration procedures, and lots of good suggestions for prepping for the tests. See pages 124 and 129.

AP, IB, and CLEP exams

Getting a head start

The last type of standardized tests you'll need to worry about are those that high school students can take to earn college credit before ever setting foot on campus.

AP (**Advanced Placement**) exams, **IB** (**International Baccalaureate**) exams, and **CLEP** (**College-Level Examination Program**) tests are optional, but if you attend a school that offers AP or IB courses and you want admission to a competitive college, you should seriously consider taking at least a few of these tests.

Fast Facts: The AP

1. AP exams are based on specific AP, or Advanced Placement, courses offered in some U.S. high schools. They're college level. If your school offers any AP courses (now available in 33 subjects), you should take them if you can handle this level of difficulty.

2. The AP exam is given once in May, at the close of the course.

3. The AP is scored on a scale from 1 to 5 (5 is the top score, 3 the "qualifying" score for most colleges). Advanced placement credit varies by college; you'll have to check each individual school to find out if you are eligible, and if so, for what sort of advanced standing.

4. To register, contact your AP teacher or AP coordinator. The fee is $77 per test, but it may be waived if you can demonstrate financial hardship.

5. To send scores, designate your colleges on your answer sheet when you take the test. Otherwise you can request your scores by phone at 609-771-7300 or by going to **www.collegeboard.com/ap/students/exam/grades**. There is a $13 fee for each transcript and a $7 additional fee for ordering by phone.

Fast Facts: The CLEP

1. CLEP stands for the College-Level Examination Program. CLEP exams allow you to earn college credit or skip entry-level courses at nearly 3,000 colleges. If you were homeschooled, took community college courses, grew up in a bilingual household, or have advanced preparation in a subject, taking a CLEP may be a good idea.

2. Nearly 40 CLEP's are offered in five general subject areas: composition and literature, foreign languages, history and social sciences, science and mathematics, and business.

3. The tests take 90 minutes, are mostly multiple choice, and have a score between 20 and 80 points. College credit varies by school; just ask.

4. To register, go to **www.collegeboard.com**. Each exam costs $50.

How to Prepare

The College Board publishes a CLEP *Official Study Guide*, plus individual guides for each subject. You can find others like Princeton Review's *Cracking the CLEP* by Tom Meltzer and Paul Foglino.

Fast Facts: The IB

1. IB's are offered in a small number (just over 400) of U.S. high schools. This challenging program was developed to serve the needs of international students, especially the children of diplomats who move frequently, but it has become popular with locals as well. Most colleges recognize the difficulty of the program and award credit.

2. IB's are under the jurisdiction of the International Baccalaureate Organization (**www.ibo.org**), which publishes extensive information about the tests and curriculum on its site. For more details, speak with your guidance counselor or IB coordinator.

3. IB courses in six subjects are taken in the junior and senior years. Most exams are taken at the end of the senior year. The exams are graded on a point system from 1 to 7, with 7 as the highest possible score.

How to Prepare

The best preparation is through course work. However, you may also order back copies of exams from the IB home page (see above).

improving your scores

Sorting through the advice

An entire industry has sprung up to help students increase their standardized test scores. The amount of money many families spend on courses, publications, and books far exceeds the cost of the test themselves—and even the cost of some colleges' yearly tuition! Take advantage of these methods, but what you do depends on how badly you want a good score, how much money you have to spend, and how much effort you can give.

Books Among the publishers are SparkNotes, Barron's, Princeton Review, the College Board, Kaplan, Peterson's, Arco, and REA. The typical format usually begins with a description of the test, test-taking strategies, and then gives practice exams and answer keys. They're all quite similar; buy one.

Online You can find free online sample tests and answers at most of the publisher sites, for example, **http://testprep.sparknotes.com**, **www.collegeboard.com**, and **www.petersons.com**.

Test prep courses See your guidance counselor for courses in your area. Most focus more on test-taking strategies than content but will include diagnostic exams to see where you need the most help. Costs vary. You can get some idea by checking out Kaplan (**www.kaptest.com**) or Princeton Review (**www.princetonreview.com/testprep**). Some schools sponsor the courses free or at a reduced fee, and there are online courses as well.

Private tutors Costs vary but can soar to hundreds of dollars an hour in big cities. Expensive isn't necessarily better. Check your tutor's background. If he or she is sponsored by a test-prep company, carefully read their refund policies. The more expensive packages may include a money-back guarantee if you don't raise your test scores by a certain number of points, provided you agree to do every bit of the assigned homework. For names, see your guidance counselor.

Test-taking Tips

Here are some things that can help you do well on the SAT and ACT. They are no substitute, however, for a good test-prep course or book.

- Familiarize yourself with the format of the test you are taking: its length, types of questions, grading policies, and levels of difficulty.
- Take the PSAT/NMSQT or PLAN practice tests to gain some sense of how you will do. Plan a personal strategy to improve, through an online prep class, an actual class, a book, or a tutor.
- Read the test prep strategies online and in your prep book.
- Take lots of sample exams, employing the test strategies above, to get used to approaching the exam in the smartest way.
- Start preparing for the SAT or ACT in January of your junior year, before taking it in the spring.
- Take practice ACT's and SAT's to see which is easier for you.
- Don't cram the night before the test; it's too late to improve your score significantly, and you'll just be tired and stressed the next day.
- Get a good night's sleep, then rise early, with plenty of time to eat.
- Give yourself enough time to make it to the test center. Check ahead of time how to get there and how long the trip takes.
- Check that you have your admission ticket and all the other materials your ticket says you should bring, including several sharpened #2 pencils with erasers, acceptable ID, and, depending on the test, a calculator, as well as extra batteries for the calculator. (You'll be given a list of acceptable types of calculators, so make sure you have the right kind.) Prepare this stuff the night before. Bring tissues, and anything else you might need.

The Answers

Keep in mind some simple advice about answering questions.

- Skipping is O.K. All questions are worth the same number of points, so if you get stuck on a hard question, move on.
- Guess! The SAT deducts a fraction of a point for wrong answers, the ACT does not. In both cases it's O.K. to guess, but do it intelligently—try eliminating obviously wrong answers first to better the odds. Using this strategy with the SAT, at the worst you'll break even; with the ACT there's no penalty at all.
- Write your answer choice in your booklet as well as on the answer sheet. This way, if you discover you've marked the wrong spots on the answer sheet, you can fix it without having to solve the problems all over again!

special needs

It's your right

All sorts of special testing accommodations are available for students who need them, whether for a physical or learning disability or **ADD** (attention deficit disorder). The trick is to find out what they are, how to apply for them, and do it early enough to benefit from them. Take it step by step and don't give up—it's your right!

Some of the possible accommodations include

- A sign-language interpreter
- Large-print books
- A wheelchair-accessible room
- Permission to bring in snacks or medications
- Extended time
- A writer to record your responses
- A reader for the questions
- A Braille edition of the test

If you need special testing accommodations, such as a sign-language interpreter, make arrangements several months ahead of whenever you plan to take your first test.

Start by finding out who at your school is responsible for working with special-needs students. Meet with that person. The staffer should be able to guide you through the process. Do this several months ahead of whenever you plan to take your first test. You can also find out most of what you need to know online. The College Board's Web site (**www.collegeboard.com**) has pages of information on securing accommodations for the SAT, PSAT, and AP. For accommodations when taking the ACT, see **www.act.org**.

Special Accommodations for the PSAT, SAT, and AP

1. Review the eligibility requirements online (**www.collegeboard.com**) and with your school counselor. You will need to have current, acceptable documentation on file in your school specifying that you have a disability requiring testing accommodations.

2. Have your school submit a request for accommodations for you. This new form, called the SSD Student Eligibility Form, has to be submitted only once to cover all the exams sponsored by the College Board.

3. If you are approved, you will receive an SSD Eligibility Letter with your own SSD Code from the College Board.

4. Register by submitting a written request via mail, attaching a copy of your SSD Eligibility Letter. As of this writing you can't register online, but the College Board is working on it, so keep checking.

Begin the process of applying for accommodations about six months ahead of taking your first exam. You have to register for these exams weeks ahead of time. Before that, you need to have your eligibility letter, which takes several more weeks. And you may need other new documentation, which will take even more time.

Special Accommodations for the ACT

1. See your school counselor, and review all the testing accommodation options and requirements at the ACT Web site, **www.act.org**.

2. For the ACT, procedures, forms, and dates vary, depending on the type of accommodations you request. Follow instructions carefully for each. As with the SAT, you will have to register on paper. Unlike the SAT, you can in most cases make your request right along with your registration, so the process is not as lengthy. But the ACT does not offer all types of accommodations on every testing date. You'll have to find the specific dates for the accommodations you need.

now what do I do?

Answers to common questions

How can I decide whether to take the SAT or the ACT?

Overall, it's a little easier to prepare for and take the exam that's most common in your part of the country (the SAT is more common in the Northeast and West, the ACT in the Midwest and South), and the one your guidance counselor and school most usually emphasize. But with everyone looking to exploit every advantage in the college admissions game, people are starting to compare these two tests. You'll find arguments for both, but you really do have the option of taking either test for just about any college. And the tests are quite different. So order a practice exam for each and try it. See how you do and which format is easier for you. Some experts suggest taking both.

How can I find colleges that don't require either the SAT or the ACT?

Go to **www.fairtest.org** for a list of nearly 400 schools that have deemphasized test scores. Some don't require them at all, others say they're optional, and some ask for them but give them much less emphasis. From this list you can check individual schools' requirements. Experts say take the tests anyway, you never know!

If the PSAT is a practice test, why take it twice?

Because when you take it in your junior year, there is a possible National Merit Scholarship riding on it. By practicing in your sophomore year, you'll have a better shot at some financing for college when you retake it. Plus taking the PSAT and PLAN allows you to enter your name into the mail system that colleges use to recruit students.

Can I take the IB exams if they're not offered at my high school?

Not generally. The IB exams are the culmination of a two-year course of study that also includes an extensive essay and community service. The tests were not designed to grant college credit the way the AP's and CLEP's were. Their purpose originally was to ensure that international college students who move frequently have a standardized curriculum that is recognized by the best international colleges. This translated into such a challenging curriculum that U.S. colleges have now begun awarding credit for IB exams, depending on how well the student scores.

For religious reasons, I can't take my tests on Saturdays. What should I do?

If you can't take the test on Saturday for religious reasons, Sunday—and some Monday—test dates are available (but only for religious reasons). You'll have to supply some documentation (such as a letter from your clergy member), but otherwise it's no big deal.

Is there a scholarship connected to the PSAT?

The second part of the PSAT's name is National Merit Scholarship Qualifying Test. Your score on the PSAT determines whether you qualify to enter into the competition for one. (If you score high enough, you will receive a scholarship application.) Your guidance counselor should have copies of the PSAT/NMSQT Student Bulletin, which describes the test and scholarship program in detail.

Now where do I go?

CONTACTS

SparkNotes
http://testprep.sparknotes.com

ACT
www.act.org

The College Board
www.collegeboard.com/testing/

Educational Testing Service
www.ets.org
Private educational testing and measurement organization.

International Baccalaureate Organization
www.ibo.org

National Center for Fair and Open Testing
www.fairtest.org/univ/optional.htm
Lists of colleges not requiring test scores for admission.

PUBLICATIONS

SparkNotes Test Preparation Guides (SAT, PSAT, ACT, and SAT II)

Gruber's Complete Preparation for the SAT

The SAT for Dummies
By Suzee J. Vlk

The ACT for Dummies
By Suzee J. Vlk

Kaplan Higher Score SAT, ACT & PSAT

The Princeton Review: Inside the SAT & ACT

Cracking the CLEP
By Tom Meltzer and Paul Foglino

Barron's How to Prepare for SAT II

The College Board 10 Real SAT's

chapter 7

If my parents save for college, won't that work against our getting a good financial aid package?

Check out page 160

Paying for college

what college costs

There's an affordable, good school out there for you

When it comes to paying for college, ignore the myths.

Myth #1 College is so expensive that only the wealthy can afford it.
Reality It's not as expensive as you think. Only several private colleges run into mind-blowing numbers ($30,000 to $40,000 per year). State schools and community colleges remain a real bargain.

Myth #2 I shouldn't apply to expensive colleges. I can't afford them.

Reality Even expensive colleges give away a lot of financial aid. Don't be discouraged by the "sticker price." Don't ever rule out a school as too expensive until you've seen the financial aid they offer.

Myth #3 College doesn't seem worth the cost. Wouldn't it be better to just get a job and start earning money right away?
Reality People with college degrees earn nearly double what people without them earn. College is the best investment you will ever make! According to the College Board and the U.S. Census Bureau, over a lifetime a college grad will earn $1 million more on average than someone without a college degree. Still breathing?

Myth #4 Financial aid benefits only the poor. The rich can afford tuition. It's the middle class that is squeezed.
Reality If your family income is at a certain level, it's true that you'll be expected to pay part of your college costs. But many private colleges award aid to well over half their students. And state schools are affordable to almost everyone. What's more, in recent years, the government has come up with some programs (for example, Education IRA's, the Hope Scholarship Credit, and the Lifetime Learning tax credit, see page 144) that are specifically aimed at helping ease the tuition burden for the middle class.

What Are Students Really Paying?

According to the College Board, nearly 70% of students at four-year colleges pay less than $8,000 for tuition, and 40% pay less than $4,000. Almost half of all college students attend community colleges, where the average tuition is under $2,000 per year.

financial aid basics

What you need to know

There are entire books dedicated to finding ways to pay for college (in fact, you should pick one of these up—see page 161). Here's what you need to know to start.

Financial aid is for everyone All students except the very wealthy are eligible for some form of financial aid. College students received a record $90 *billion* in financial aid in 2002. The biggest chunk comes from the federal government. But to receive it, you must apply for it.

You can't do this alone. You need your parents Colleges assume you are a dependent of your parents, so your financial aid package will be based upon their financial situation, as well as any income or savings you may have. They will have to fill out forms in order for you to be eligible and will be expected to contribute to the cost of your education. So keep them involved and aware of deadlines.

You have help College applications come with detailed instructions about applying for financial aid. Your guidance counselor should be able to steer you through the process. You should also stay in close touch with the financial aid officers at the colleges to which you are applying. They are the experts and are there to help, so call and ask questions. Finally, if your parents use an accountant or tax preparer, they should consult with that person, too.

There are three basic kinds of financial aid

- **Grants and scholarships, or gift aid** Money that you don't have to pay back.

- **Loans** Someday you'll have to pay this money back (usually after graduation), but the **interest rates** (fees that are a percentage of the total amount you borrowed and that you have to pay in addition to repaying the actual loan) are much lower than a typical bank loan.

- **Work study** You work a certain number of hours per week (usually 10 to 20) on campus for a salary to offset your college costs.

There are three main sources for financial aid

These sources are the federal government, state governments, and colleges themselves. (Private scholarships, although numerous, represent less than 5% of the total financial aid awarded.)

Applying for financial aid is actually pretty simple

The main thing you and your parents have to do to apply for financial aid is to fill out and submit the Free Application for Federal Student Aid (**FAFSA**) as early as possible after January 1 but before March 2. For some colleges you'll need to submit the College Scholarship Service Profile financial aid form (CSS Profile), or the college's own aid form. If you need help, see your high school guidance counselor or a college financial aid counselor.

grants and scholarships

Free money

Grants and scholarships are also known as gift aid, since they do not have to be repaid. There are three main types of government grants available: Pell Grants, Supplemental Educational Opportunity Grants (SEOG), and State Student Incentive Grants (SSIG).

Federal grants, like all other federal aid, are **need-based**. In other words, they are based upon your family's ability to pay. Many colleges also offer **merit scholarships** based upon some sort of achievement. Sometimes merit scholarships come with strings attached—you may have to maintain a certain average or play a certain sport.

Don't worry, you won't have to apply separately for each one. Just fill out the required financial aid form (the FAFSA and/or CSS Profile) and the college will put together a package that includes any grants or scholarships for which you are eligible. If there is additional paperwork, they will guide you through it after you've accepted their offer.

Institutional Grants and Scholarships

Nearly 20% of all financial grants and scholarships come from the colleges themselves. At private colleges these awards can be very large. When you apply to each college, you will be considered for any available grants or scholarships they have. Most are need-based, but some are based on merit.

Big Money from Big Government

There are three main types of federal aid.

Pell Grants are distributed through a huge federal grant program directed at low-income students. While the amount changes, the maximum grant is between $3,000 and $4,000.

The **Supplemental Educational Opportunity Grant Program** (SEOG) is another federal grant program for low-income students; it supplements Pell Grants. The college must pay a percentage of the grant.

State Student Incentive Grants (SSIGs) are federal awards to states to create their own grant programs. Many states have their own scholarships, both need-based and otherwise, so talk to your financial aid officer or guidance counselor. See the Web site of your state department of education for more information.

private scholarships

Researching awards, spotting scams

While the bulk of financial aid is awarded through colleges and the government (see pages 146-149), there are lots of private scholarships that you can go after yourself. Should you?

Yes, even though in some cases the college will deduct this amount from your overall financial aid package. You may wind up with the same amount of money, but scholarships look good on a résumé. Plus, if you are enrolling in a school that gives little aid, or if you are not eligible for much aid, a scholarship helps. Or if your financial aid package consists mostly of loans, the scholarship will offset money you would have to pay back.

Check in your community about scholarships from civic or charitable groups. Ask your parents if their employers offer scholarships for family members. Search online for private scholarships. For example, go to the Foundation Center at **www.fdncenter.org** and under "finding funder," click on "grantmaker" Web sites and select "corporate" grantmakers. Search by entering the word "scholarship" and you'll see a list of more than 50 corporations that give awards with links on how to apply. Or go to **www.fastweb.com** for financial aid information and a free scholarship search.

Apply for everything that interests you, even if you think your chances are not good. You just never know.

ASK THE EXPERTS

Who gives out private scholarships, and why?

Everyone from employers to small charitable organizations gives out scholarships. Eligibility may be based on academics, athletic or musical skill, race, gender, disability, religion, or career interest. Private scholarships represent about 5% of the aid awarded each year. Also apply for aid from the government and the colleges themselves (see pages 146–149), which represents much more—95% of annual aid.

Should I pay to do a scholarship search?

No. All reputable online scholarship searches are free. You can do your own research online. For starters, try the scholarship searches at the College Board Web site (**www.collegeboard.com**), the Princeton Review (**www.review.com**), Peterson's (**www.petersons.com**), FastAid, at **www.fastaid.com**, FinAid, the Smart Student's Guide to Financial Aid, at **www.finaid.org**, and FastWeb at **www.fastweb.com**. These sites sift through anywhere from 200,000 to more than a million awards. But beware: There are also many scams out there. You will find them online, in your mailbox, and on your phone.

What does a scholarship scam look like?

Mail scams are common. You receive an official-looking letter from an organization with an "official" sounding name like the National Financial Aid Group. It says you have an appointment at a hotel or conference center for financial aid. This is a come-on to get you to show up and pay for some service. Avoid any company that guarantees a scholarship. Never give away bank account or credit card information over the phone to someone offering to do scholarship searches for you. If you have any doubts about such offers, talk to your college counselor.

loans

Borrowing your tuition

Monthly payments for tuition loans generally start sometime within a year after you finish college and are spread out over several years. Loan information changes regularly, so check for current details with your guidance counselor and the financial aid officers at the colleges where you applied. Plans vary in **interest rates** and **repayment plans**. Interest rates are the fees you pay to borrow money. The interest rate for a loan is a percentage of the amount you borrowed (known as the **principal). Repayment plans** are monthly payments to pay off your loan, including both the principal and interest.

Loans for students

Subsidized Stafford Loans These loans are based upon need and carry an interest rate that is capped at 8.25%. "Subsidized" means that the government will cover the cost of your interest payments while you are in college. Funds for Stafford loans come from two government sources: the Federal Family Education Loan program (FFEL) or the William D. Ford Direct Student Loan program (DSL). They are nearly identical in terms, but FFEL funds are funneled by the government to students through private lenders like banks. With Direct Student Loans, the government gives the money directly to the colleges.

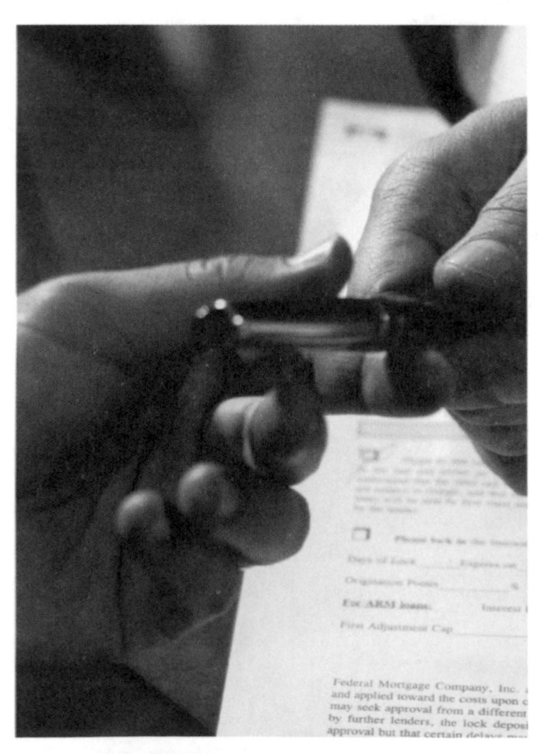

Unsubsidized Stafford Loans Unsubsidized Stafford loans carry the same 8.25% cap on interest, but you are responsible for paying the interest that builds up on your loan while you are in college. You do not have to demonstrate need to receive an unsubsidized loan. If your financial aid package isn't enough and your parents are tapped out, you can borrow more yourself through this program.

Perkins Loan This program provides low-interest (even lower, at 5%) loans for the most needy students. Perkins Loans are financed partly by the federal government, partly by the colleges, and partly by repayments from former recipients.

Loans for parents

PLUS Loans These unsubsidized Parent Loans for Undergraduate Students are available either from FFEL, in which case the college will pass your parents' application on to a private lender, and they will make payments to that lender, or from DSL. If the loan is from DSL, the funds go to the college directly from the Department of Education, the lender. Interest rates for PLUS loans are capped at 9%. Your parents don't have to demonstrate need. To qualify, they must have a good **credit rating**—a history of how they used credit and made payments—to determine the likelihood of their repaying a loan.

ASK THE EXPERTS

What are Nellie Mae and Sallie Mae?

They're the country's largest providers of education loans to parents and students. Originally separate companies, Sallie Mae, formally known as the SLM Corp., purchased Nellie Mae in 1999.

What are consolidation loans?

Available through both FFEL and DSL, and for both subsidized and unsubsidized loans, these let you combine all your education loans into one loan, usually at the same or sometimes even at a lower rate of interest. You then make only one monthly payment.

work study

Trading hours for tuition

One way to work your way to a degree is through a **work-study** job. It's not a loan, but if you qualify you work 10 to 20 hours a week, usually on campus. In exchange, your salary helps pay down college expenses. It's available through a federal program that gives a certain amount of money each year to colleges to use for student employment.

If you are eligible for aid, you will probably be given a work-study assignment as part of your financial aid package.

The jobs typically assume your work, of 10 to 20 hours per week, will be worth around $2,800 a year. Jobs are usually on campus, in offices like the admissions or development office doing clerical work, or working in the library, dining hall, or dorms, or in theater services.

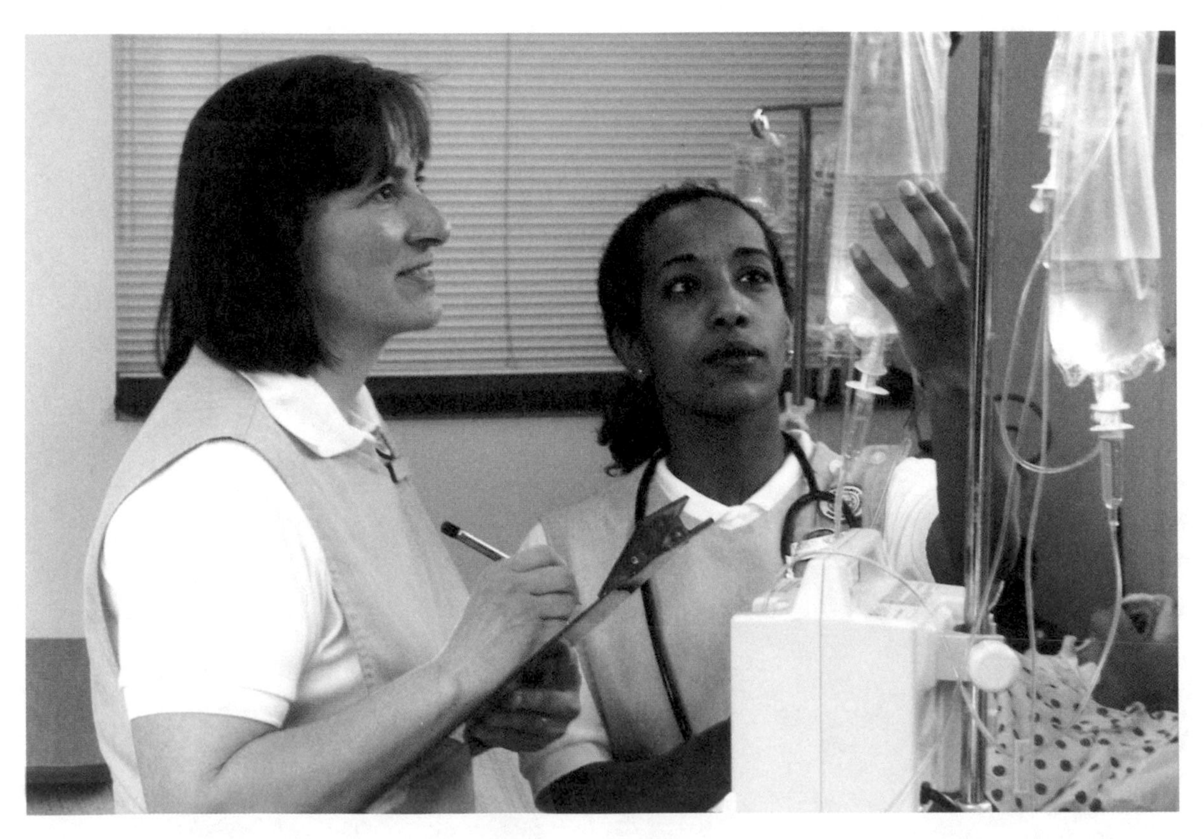

Can I change jobs if I don't like the one I get?

Sure, if another slot is available. Apply early. The best jobs go fast.

What if I find a job that pays more money?

If you can find another job that pays better, take it and decline work study. The college always has students looking for work study.

How do I know where I'll end up working?

It depends on the college. You may go to the college's financial aid office, select a job, and confirm the arrangements with the appropriate office, or the college may assign you a job.

FIRST PERSON SUCCESS STORY

Working and Networking

At first I was definitely depressed about having a work-study job. I mean, how was I supposed to fit working into my schedule of classes—not to mention parties! But it was actually no big deal. First of all, the work was pretty easy. (I was a receptionist for the chemistry department—how hard was that? Sometimes I even got my homework done there.) Plus I really got an insider's view of the way the college was run. But the best part is that I really got to know some of the professors and administrators, which came in handy when I wanted to do research with one particular teacher. The head of the chemistry department recommended me and even took me over and introduced me.

—Brenda J., Chicago

tax breaks

Uncle Sam can help

Just giving money to you isn't the only way the government can help you pay for college. Here are some income tax credits for you and your parents, plus special savings plans that let you set aside money to help pay for a college education. Check with a college financial officer for any change in the tax law.

Freshman and sophomore years

The **Hope Scholarship Credit** lets parents take a **tax credit** (a reduction in taxes owed) of up to $1,500 each year for the first two years of college. The way it works is that taxpayers take a credit equal to the first $1,000 spent on tuition and other college expenses, then 50 cents on the dollar for the next $1,000, up to the maximum of $1,500 each year.

Any year

The **Lifetime Learning Credit** is for any year of undergraduate or graduate study. Each student takes a tax credit equal to 20% of the first $5,000 (or up to $1,000) of college expenses. Beginning in January 2003, the credit increases to as much as 20% of the first $10,000, or up to $2,000. Check with a college financial aid office for the latest details.

In each case, your parent must owe taxes to be eligible for the credit. If they owe less than the credit, they will not receive a refund for the difference. Parents should speak with an accountant or tax preparer to make sure they take full advantage of these programs and to find out about any changes that may affect you.

Planning to Save

The old-fashioned way to finance college is to save for it. (Don't worry if your parents don't have enough to cover it all, very few do.) Two tax breaks encourage savings.

- **Coverdell Education Savings Account** Your parents can contribute $2,000 a year per child. Money earned on that investment is federal tax–free if it's used toward college. For income levels up to $110,000 if filing singly and up to $220,000 if filing jointly.

529 Plan Offered by individual states, it comes in two forms:

- **College savings plan** Your parents can save as much money as they want in a state-managed fund. The money they earn is tax-free for qualified college expenses. The money can be used to pay for the college of your choice. The tax law is scheduled to change in 2011, so check with a college financial aid office or a college financial planner for how it may impact you.

- **Prepaid tuition plan** It locks in today's tuition rates, which is a huge savings. If your parents sign on, however, you will probably be required to attend certain schools.

If your state doesn't have one of these plans, check out **www.collegesavings.org** for other college saving plans. For more, see **www.collegeboard.com** and click on "paying for college." Also see **www.savingforcollege.com**.

how to apply

Start by asking Uncle Sam

The Free Application for Federal Student Aid, or **FAFSA**, represents almost one-stop shopping in applying for financial aid.

Get a FAFSA form from your guidance counselor in November or December, or you can find and file it online at **www.fafsa.ed.gov**. Do this early and ask your parents to read it. Like a tax form, it will take some time to complete. When you and your parents obtain the form, fill it out and send it in as soon as possible after January 1 (no earlier is allowed). Your parents will have to provide their income tax information.

Why their income tax? Because most financial aid is based upon your parents' income. After income, investments and other assets are considered. Your parents should request their W2 forms from their employers right after January 1. Because timing is important, they can initially estimate their income and submit any corrections later. Processing of paper forms takes about four weeks, online processing about two weeks. Financial aid, while based on need, tends to be first come, first served. There's a limited pot of money for aid, so the sooner you apply, the better.

Filling Out the FAFSA Form

You can apply by mail, which takes about four weeks to process, or on the Web, which takes about two. You may have to mail in a signature page before the form can be processed. The Web site (**www.fafsa.ed.gov**) and the form itself have extensive instructions. Other Web sites, such as the College Board, **www.collegeboard.com**, also have excellent instructions. Most guidance counselors and college financial aid officers can steer you through, and if your parents use an accountant, have that person help. If you still have questions, call the Federal Student Aid Information Center at 800-433-3243.

FAFSA on the Web

Home | Pin Site | Help | Contact Us | FAQs | Site Map

Discover Your Opportunities! | Before Beginning a FAFSA | Filling Out a FAFSA | FAFSA Follow-Up

Overview
General Student Aid Info
Documents Needed
Pre-Application Worksheet
Drug Conviction Worksheet
Interactive Worksheets

Before Beginning a FAFSA Overview

Time Saving Suggestions

Get documents you need
Start with your Social Security Number, driver's license, income tax return, bank statements and investment records.

Print a Pre-Application Worksheet

72. If your parents have filed or will file a 1040, were they eligible to file a

For questions 73 - 83, if the answer is zero or the question does not apply, enter 0.

73. What was your parents' adjusted gross income for 2001? Adjusted gross income is on IRS Form 1040–line 33; 1040A–line 19; 1040EZ–line 4; or Telefile–line I. $ ___ , ___

74. Enter the total amount of your parents' income tax for 2001. Income tax amount is on IRS Form 1040–lines 47 + 52; 1040A–lines 30 + 34; 1040EZ–line 11; or Telefile–line K(2). $ ___ , ___

75. Enter your parents' exemptions for 2001. Exemptions are on IRS Form 1040–line 6d or on Form 1040A–line 6d. For Form 1040EZ or Telefile, **see page 2.** ___

76-77. How much did your parents earn from working (wages, salaries, tips, etc.) in 2001? Answer this question whether or not your parents filed a tax return. This information may be on their W-2 forms, or on IRS Form 1040–lines 7 + 12 + 18; 1040A–line 7; or 1040EZ–line 1. Telefilers should use their W-2 forms.
Father/ Stepfather (76) $ ___ , ___
Mother/ Stepmother (77) $ ___ , ___

Parent Worksheets (78-80)

78-80. Go to page 8 and complete the columns on the right of Worksheets A, B, and C. Enter the parent totals in questions 78, 79, and 80, respectively. Even though your parents may have few of the worksheet items, check each line carefully.
Worksheet A (78) $ ___ , ___
Worksheet B (79) $ ___ , ___
Worksheet C (80) $ ___ , ___

81. As of today, what is the net worth of your parents' current **investments**? **See page 2.** $ ___ , ___

82. As of today, what is the net worth of your parents' current **businesses and/or investment farms**? **See page 2**. Do not include a farm that your parents live on and operate. $ ___ , ___

83. As of today, what is your parents' total current balance of **cash, savings, and checking accounts**? $ ___ , ___

Now go to Step Six.

Source: www.fafsa.ed.gov

how to apply, part 2

What private colleges want to know

Some colleges (about 600, usually private schools) don't think FAFSA gives an accurate picture of your family's finances, so they require a different form, the **Profile.** The Profile can take other assets, like **home equity** (the cash value of your house minus the mortgage you still owe on it) into account. Some particularly picky colleges even have their own forms. Check with each of the colleges on your list to see what forms they require. You have to register before you can apply for the Profile, because it creates a customized application for you. When registering, you list all the colleges you want your Profile sent to, and when you receive your application it will ask only the questions those specific colleges want answered. You can register online, which generates an online application (faster and easier), or by phone to receive a paper application.

Online Go to the College Board (**www.collegeboard.com**), click on "paying for college," then CSS/Profile online.

By phone Get a copy of the Profile Registration Guide from your guidance counselor, fill it out, then call 800-778-6888. Unlike the government form, the Profile is not free. It's $5 to register online, $7 by phone, and $17 for each college you want the information sent to.

After registering, you'll receive your customized application online or in the mail. Fill out the information and send it in. All the colleges on your list will receive it.

HELP SITE SEARCH SHOP ABOUT US

PLANNING FOR COLLEGE | TAKING THE TESTS | FINDING THE RIGHT COLLEGE | GETTING INTO COLLEGE | PAYING FOR COLLEGE | MY ORGANIZER

START PAGE | SAT REG. & SCORES | SAT PREP | COLLEGE LIST | COLLEGE APPLICATIONS | CSS/PROFILE

collegeboard.com

VeriSign Secure Site Click to verify

VISA MasterCard AMEX

Paying for College > CSS/PROFILE

CSS/Financial Aid PROFILE®

The fast, easy, convenient, secure way to apply for financial aid

Welcome to PROFILE, the financial aid application service of the College Board -- a national, 100-year-old, not-for-profit membership association. Many of the member colleges, universities, graduate and professional schools, and scholarship programs use the information collected on PROFILE to help them award nonfederal student aid funds. Also ... for the Imaging & Documentation S... (IDOC™) is available from this site.

Section I - Parents' Assets

If parents own all or part of a business or farm, enter its name and the percent of ownership in Section P

37. Cash, savings, and checking accounts (as of today)

38. a Total value of assets held in the names of the student's brothers and sisters who are under age 19 and not college students $

b Total value of assets held in Section 529 prepaid tuition plans for the student's brothers and sisters $

c Total value of assets held in Section 529 prepaid tuition plans for the student $

39. Investments

What is it worth today? $

What is owed on it? $

40. Home

a What is it worth today? (Renters fill in "0" and skip to 40d.) $

What is owed on it? $

b Year purchased

c Purchase price $

d Monthly home mortgage or rental payment (If none, explain in Section P) $

41. Business

What is it worth today? $

What is owed on it? $

42. Farm

a What is it worth today? $

What is owed on it? $

b Does family live on the farm? O Yes O No

Sample. Do Not Use.

43. Other real estate

a What is it worth today? $

What is owed on it? $

b Year purchased

c Purchase price $

Section J - Parents' 2001 Income & Benefits

44. 2001 Adjusted Gross Income (IRS Form 1040, line 33 or 1040A, line 19 or 1040EZ, line 4 or Telefile, line I) $

45. 2001 U.S. income tax paid (IRS Form 1040, line 52 or, 1040A, line 34 or 1040EZ, line 11 or Telefile, line K) $

46. 2001 itemized deductions (IRS Form 1040, Schedule A, line 28. Enter "0" if deductions were not itemized.) $

47. 2001 untaxed income and benefits (Include the same types of income that are listed in 55 a-k.) $

Source: CSS/Financial Aid PROFILE, www.collegeboard.com. Reprinted with permission.

what you pay

Your contribution

Within two to four weeks after you submit the FAFSA, the federal aid form, you should receive your **Student Aid Report**, or SAR. Look for your **Expected Family Contribution (EFC),** the amount your family is expected to pay. When you submit your Profile form, you will learn your **Expected Family Contribution amount.** Note this, because it may be higher or lower than what the government expected your family to pay. Colleges that rely on Profile information will use the Profile figure, not the Student Aid Report figure.

If there are mistakes, correct them now by going to the FAFSA Web site or speaking with your guidance counselor. Some schools will submit corrections for you.

How the Numbers Work

Tuition	College 1	$ 10,000	College 2	$ 4,000
Your EFC		$ 6,000		$ 6,000
College aid you need		$ 4,000		None

Are there any ways to lower my EFC?

Once your EFC has been determined, based on the information you file with the FAFSA and your CSS Profile, it is unlikely you can change it. You can try to negotiate with the financial aid office of the college after you receive your package, however, if you feel there are mitigating circumstances (the recent loss of a job, for example).

What can I do to affect my EFC beforehand?

The EFC is based on parental income from January 1 of your junior year to December 30 of your senior year. The way your parents report their income and assets affects your EFC. Does this mean a parent should quit a job so you can have more aid? No, that would be crazy. For detailed advice on arriving at the most favorable EFC, check out the Princeton Review's Web site section on paying for college, and click on "financial aid and your tax return" (**www.princetonreview.com/college/finance/articles/save/aidandtax.asp**). See an accountant or financial planner who specializes in college aid.

Will my EFC change from year to year?

No, not if your family finances stay the same. But if more of your siblings start attending college, your EFC should go down.

Whom should I call to figure out my SAR (Student Aid Report)?

You can contact the Federal Student Aid Information Center at 319-337-5665. They have counselors who can help you with financial aid programs, the status of your FAFSA, and financial aid questions.

Can I appeal to the college for more money?

Sometimes, especially if you face new circumstances or withheld some information for reasons of privacy or pride. Perhaps your family develops sudden, overwhelming medical expenses or a parent loses a job. Be gracious. Also be prepared: Some schools do not negotiate.

weighing the risks

When asking for aid hurts your chances

You may wonder if your need for financial aid will affect a college's decision about whether to admit you. The short answer is, sometimes.

Some colleges use a **need-blind** policy for their admissions decisions. This means that admissions decisions are made without regard to your financial situation. If the college admits you, its financial aid office will offer you a package of aid to attend that school.

Other colleges, however, have a **need-sensitive**, or **need-aware**, admissions policy. This means that your financial situation could influence whether you are admitted. Usually, this affects only students who are borderline. In other words, if a college is considering its bottom tier of students and one needs a lot of money but another doesn't, the preference may go to the one who needs less.

Top students, which every college wants, don't have to worry as much. Colleges will usually cover the expenses of top students in order to induce them to attend.

You can find out which system a college uses at its Web site, in a general college guidebook, or on a college guide Web site.

ASK THE EXPERTS

What is preferential packaging?

Preferential packaging is another tactic colleges (even those with supposedly need-blind admissions) use. In this case, while on the surface the aid packages may add up to the same amount, the more desirable student may be given a greater proportion of money in the form of scholarships and grants, while the other will receive mainly loans that have to be repaid.

If I have a poor academic record, is it better not to ask for financial aid?

Few parents can afford to pay the full cost of college, so if you want to go you will probably have to apply for aid and hope for the best. If you apply to schools with need-blind admissions, at the very least you won't be accepted or rejected based upon your financial situation. And while top students may win the best packages, most schools will still try to meet some or all of your financial need. Apply to several schools so you can compare financial aid packages and accept the best offer.

the aid package

Understanding what a school has to offer

After the admissions office at a college decides to accept you, it notifies the financial aid office, which then comes up with a financial aid package for you. You will receive an award letter that comes either with your acceptance packet or shortly thereafter.

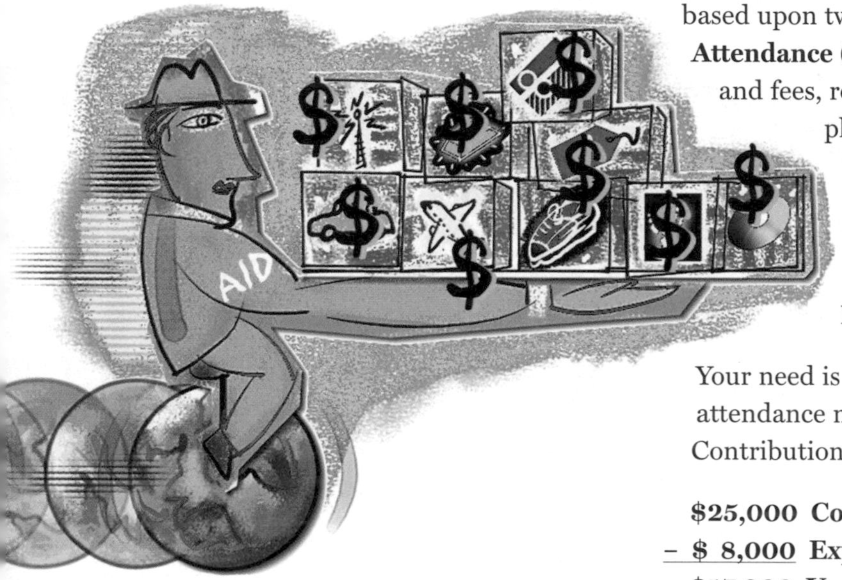

The college's financial aid package will be calculated based upon two numbers. First, the **Cost of Attendance** (COA) is the total cost of tuition and fees, room and board, books and supplies, travel and personal expenses. Next, the **Expected Family Contribution** (EFC) is the amount your family is expected to pay, calculated either by the FAFSA or Profile financial aid form.

Your need is calculated like this: Cost of attendance minus your Expected Family Contribution equals your need.

$25,000	**Cost of attendance**
– $ 8,000	**Expected Family Contribution**
$17,000	**Your need**

To meet your need, the college will typically put together a package of several types of aid, usually a combination of grants or scholarships, loans, and work study. Packages vary, even among students with similar finances, but this is the norm. Read everything you receive from the college's financial aid office. If there's anything you don't understand, contact that office.

The Package Worksheet

	Your Numbers		Example
Grants and Scholarships	___________		$ 10,000
+			
Loans	___________	+	$ 5,000
+			
Federal Work Study (FWS)	___________	+	$ 2,000
Total Aid	___________		$ 17,000
Cost of Attendance	___________		$ 25,000
Minus Total Aid	___________	–	$ 17,000
Your Expected Family Contribution	___________		$ 8,000

It's Automatic

Remember, once you submit the federal student aid form, FAFSA, you will automatically be considered for any government aid you are eligible for, and the college will consider you for any of its grants and scholarships. You may also have to submit the Profile form, but you don't have to apply separately for any of these forms of aid.

comparing offers

Side-by-side review

Once you've received all your offers, compare them to see which is best for you. Here are some things to consider.

- Is there any unmet need? How will you find that money? (See page 158 for suggestions.)
- What is the percentage of gift aid compared to loans? How much will you have to pay back eventually?
- How much debt will you actually incur? Can you handle it?
- What are the interest rates on your various loans? A smaller loan with a higher interest rate could actually cost you more in the long run than a larger loan with a lower interest rate. Figure out the total cost of each loan—including interest—to see how much each college will actually cost.

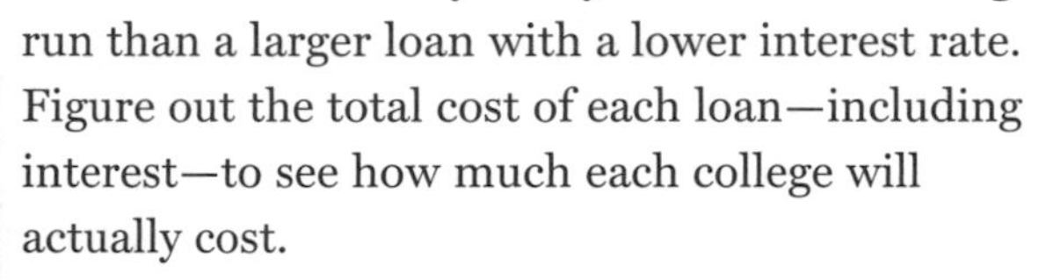

- What are the requirements for the continuation of a scholarship? Maintaining a grade point average, or something else?

For more help in comparing aid packages, check out the Princeton Review Web site (at **www.review.com**, click on "college," then "paying for college") or the College Board's Web site (**www.collegeboard.com**, click on "paying for college," then click on "receiving aid" and "paying the bill"). Both of these sites offer online comparisons of your awards. You plug in the numbers from your various award packages, see a side-by-side comparison, and are provided lots of valuable detailed advice.

If you miss the deadline for responding to your financial aid offer, your money may go to someone else. Keep copies of all your financial aid papers for reference.

ASK THE EXPERTS

Do parents or students pay back loans?

By law, the student is responsible for repayment of all student loans. The parents are responsible only for repaying any loans they take out directly, like PLUS loans. Talk about repayment with your parents. If you think they are going to help you repay your loans, clarify that. Some parents want to help as much as possible. Others view their child's repaying of a loan as a rite of passage into adulthood and responsibility.

I've settled on a college and am ready to accept their financial aid package. Can I still try to get more aid?

You will have to approach the college tactfully, but if you feel you have a good case, it's O.K. to try. Lots of people do. It's especially reasonable if your financial situation has changed since you applied for aid. But recognize that some colleges will not negotiate.

I don't want to accept all the loans in my college's financial aid package. Can I turn some down?

You need to sign off on each part of the offer individually. So if you don't want to accept some part of the package, you can decline that provision, but then it's up to you to figure out how to fill in the gap.

smart financial aid tips

How to cut tuition costs

If you're still feeling the pinch, don't lose hope—there are other ways you can control costs.

CLEP, AP, and IB These advanced placement tests may earn you college credit—every credit is a savings. Check with each college to see what they accept (see page 122).

Monthly payment plans Some colleges offer a monthly payment plan, so you can spread the cost throughout the year, just as you do when buying a computer or a piece of furniture.

Employee tuition plans Your parents may work for a company that offers tuition assistance. Ask them to check with their human resources department.

Accelerated degrees Some colleges have programs in which you can finish your B.A. in three years. Ask the admissions office. Summer school and other interim term courses can earn you a degree sooner and cut your cost of living and tuition.

Borrowing from assets Your parents may choose to borrow against their home, life insurance policy, or from retirement funds like an IRA, a Keogh, or, in some cases, a 401(k). They should check with an accountant to figure out what makes the best sense.

Your Time Can Be Money

There are several ways to trade some of your postgraduation time for college cash and help serve your country.

Military service Attend a military service academy and you'll receive your degree in exchange for serving in the military. Get an ROTC scholarship while you go to school. Or join the military and take advantage of the GI Bill to win tuition benefits either during your service or after you complete it. See page 36 and **www.gibill.va.gov**.

Peace Corps You can defer college loan payments while you're in the Peace Corps.

AmeriCorps AmeriCorps members perform public service for 10 to 12 months, usually after graduation, and in return receive a scholarship or use the funds to repay federal loans. Check out this program at **www.americorps.org**.

ASK THE EXPERTS

How do monthly payment plans work?

Instead of requiring you to pay for college costs at the beginning of each semester, some schools offer monthly payment plans, for eight, nine, or ten months. The longer plans start earlier, perhaps in May or June, but they reduce the monthly payment amount. Beware: Some colleges may offer to deduct the cost from a credit card automatically. However, unless your parents have enough income to pay off a large monthly credit card bill, the astronomical interest rates on credit cards make this a bad idea. Your parents would be better off with a PLUS loan and its 9% capped rate of interest.

Are there other ways to pay for college?

You could take a job. But be careful not to work so many hours that your grades suffer.

now what do I do?

Answers to common questions

If I ask for financial aid, will this hurt my chance for admission?

In some borderline cases, yes, a school may select a student who can pay instead of one who needs financial assistance. Look for schools that have a need-blind policy (see page 152). This means they select the students they want without considering whether they can pay the tuition. Only after admission does the school look at the student's ability to pay and consider financial aid.

If my parents save for college, won't this work against our being offered a good financial aid package?

This is a common misunderstanding. While savings and assets play a role in financial aid, most aid is calculated by looking at a parent's income (see pages 146-147).

I don't think I'm eligible for aid, so why should I apply?

In almost every case, everyone should apply. The FAFSA is free—and is also needed to qualify for some of the good unsubsidized loan rates. You may be surprised. Most people are eligible for some form of aid.

What if I can't make my loan payments?

If you are experiencing economic hardship, you can often have payments deferred for as long as three years. Most college loans give you a grace period of usually about six months after you leave school to find a job, but if you still aren't on your feet, appeal to the lender. Other reasons you might use to defer payment are military service, graduate school, disability, or participation in a program like the Peace Corps. The one thing you don't want to do is default on your loan. This means you don't pay, you don't contact the lender to work something out, and they have to come after you. In that case, you run the risk of being given a poor credit record, which could have an impact for years to come—say when you go looking for a mortgage on a house or an apartment to rent.

Help! I can't figure out how to fill out this FAFSA. What can I do?

You can find help online at **www.ed.gov/prog_info/SFA/FAFSA**, a government site with specific information about completing the FAFSA, or call 800-433-3243. Your college counselor should also be able to answer your questions. Some give seminars or tip sheets to parents to help.

What can I do if my parents can't, or won't, pay?

Ask your high school counselor about the stringent rules to qualify for independent status. If you have very unusual circumstances, you can appeal to the college's financial aid office for special consideration. You may need a letter of verification from a religious professional, a social worker, or other similar contacts.

Now where do I go?

CONTACTS

Sallie Mae
www.salliemae.com

Nellie Mae
www.nelliemae.com

Peterson's
www.petersons.com/finaid

Students.gov
www.students.gov
U.S. government financial aid and other services accessible to students

Education tax cuts
www.ed.gov/updates/97918tax.html

College Savings Plans
www.collegesavings.org/

www.savingforcollege.com

PUBLICATIONS

The Princeton Review's Paying for College Without Going Broke
By Kalman A. Chany and Geoff Martz

Don't Miss Out: The Ambitious Student's Guide to Financial Aid
By Anna Leider and Robert Leider

The College Board College Cost and Financial Aid Handbook 2002

The College Board Scholarship Handbook 2002

J.K. Lasser's Winning Ways to Save for College: Pay for College Without Breaking the Bank
By Barbara Wagner

The DK Financial Aid for College
By Ronald W. Johnson and Marc Robinson

The Complete Idiot's Guide to Financial Aid for College
By David Rye and Marc Robinson

Kiplinger's Financing College
By Kristin Davis

Financial Aid Officers: What They Do—To You and For You
By Donald Moore

Student Guide to Financial Aid
Order a free copy at
800-433-3243
www.ed.gov/offices/OPE

The College Board's Parents' Guide to Paying for College
By Gerald Krefetz

chapter 8

If I don't start college the fall after my senior year, how can I finish in four years?
Check out page 172

decision time

you're accepted!

Weighing offers, watching deadlines

Good news! The waiting is over, the answers are in, and you have several acceptances. How do you decide?

If you've made a campus visit to each college, you may already know which school you prefer. If so and you've been accepted there, the answer is clear, assuming the financial aid package meets your needs. But if you don't have a strong first choice, there are some things you can do that will help you make a decision.

Compare financial aid offers Rank them according to cost, and see page 156 for how to compare the various aid packages. If there is a school you simply cannot afford no matter what, you will have to rule it out.

But for schools where there is a manageable difference, don't let the aid package totally dictate your decision. If you will be happier at one school than another and in the long run it meets your academic, personal, and career goals better, it may well be worth the higher cost.

Visit the schools If you haven't visited all the schools you are considering, now is the time. Or maybe you need to revisit one or two, and even spend the night there. Review the advice about visiting schools on pages 44 and 58.

Revisit your criteria Some students find they've changed a lot from the beginning to the end of their senior year. Maybe some things (like being on the beach or 3,000 miles away from your parents) don't seem as important as they did several months ago. Try making a list of your criteria now—academic, social, geographic (all the categories in Chapter 3). What's most important to you now? Think about how the colleges that have accepted you meet your needs today.

Accepting an Offer

For most schools, the deadline for responding to an admissions offer is May 1, known as Candidate's Reply Date. After that, you could very well lose your place. So while it's important to take your time and make the right decision, don't miss the boat.

At schools with rolling admissions, the deadline for responding to an acceptance offer may vary (it certainly will if you apply in late April or later). A date should be included in the admissions offer, but if not, call and ask the admissions office how long you have to decide. Because they operate on a first-come, first-served basis, you need to know exactly how much time you have.

- For whichever school you accept, make sure you also send your acceptance of their financial aid offer in on time. Check the award letter—it should have a deadline, too.

- Send in the housing application promptly. Not all schools commit to providing housing for all students, so have yours in among the earliest.

- Be considerate. Take the time to decline your other offers. This way the colleges you won't be attending can admit wait-listed students.

- Include your deposit, a frequently forgotten item.

Stay Calm!

There's no one right choice. There are many great colleges out there. If you've been careful about where you applied, you will probably be happy at any of the schools that accepted you. So don't feel too burdened by this decision. Once you've made a choice, proceed with confidence, make friends, join clubs, and sign up for classes that interest you.

rejected?

You can still hit the books next fall

Your worst nightmare has come true. Only skinny, nasty little envelopes, no big, fat happy packets in the mail. It shouldn't happen to anyone, but once in a while it does. What to do? First, cry, be angry, and get it out of your system. You're entitled! It's a lot of work to put those applications together, and you put yourself on the line. Take heart and try to find out what went wrong:

- Don't take rejection personally. Colleges look for a mix of students. You may have been a fine candidate, but they may simply have had too many applicants like you (from your school or region, for instance) or wanted more music or science majors.

- On the other hand, maybe there are parts of your application package that you need to reconsider. Talk to your guidance counselor. If you can swallow your pride, call up admissions officers at the colleges that rejected your application. They may suggest revisions or a school that's a better match.

- Look at the schools you selected. Were there too many highly selective schools? If you're still seeking a status school, consider applying to a less selective school and transferring later.

Step by Step

Apply a Second Time

If you've been rejected, you still have time to apply to different schools that have **rolling admissions**—where you can apply at any time as long as they have openings.

1. See your guidance counselor and try to come up quickly with a short list of schools having rolling admissions that meet your criteria, and where you would be a good fit. Some of the college profile books, like *The College Board College Handbook*, have an index of schools with rolling admissions.

2. Call each school and ask if they are still taking applications. If so, schedule a visit and download their application off the Web.

3. Find out if there is still financial aid available. If so, find out what each school requires—do they have their own forms? Do they accept the College Board's Profile form? You'll also need to have your Student Aid Report (SAR, page 150) from your FAFSA sent.

4. Visit the school. Read all the literature first, see an admissions counselor, take a tour—just as before. If you like the school, remember to follow up with a card thanking the admissions counselor for the interview and saying how much you'd like to attend.

5. If you can, take your completed application with you on your visit. Because you have been through this process before, it should be easy. However, if there are any aspects of your application that need fixing, like your essay, do so. If you had low SAT scores and want to try again, make sure you can supply your new scores by the school's deadline. (There is a "rush" option for sending scores.) Make sure you also have copies of your recommendations and transcripts sent. Ask that they be sent quickly.

6. With rolling admissions, you usually receive an answer to your completed application within two to three weeks. So stay alert and if you don't hear, call. Let them know how interested you are.

wait-listed

Should you stay on hold?

Wait-listed? Welcome to limbo land! You've met the college's admissions requirements and they haven't rejected you, but they haven't given you a place either. They're simply waiting to see if they'll have room. Unfortunately, you have to wait, too.

When you are on a wait list, there are no guarantees. Each college has its own policies: Some rank the list, but many don't; some pick and choose to meet certain goals of the school (like achieving gender balance); some take lots of students from the wait list, but others take few or none.

Here are some things to consider when deciding whether to wait it out.

- Do you have other acceptances? If the answer is yes, you must accept a school from among those that admitted you and make a nonrefundable deposit. It's the only way to protect yourself and make sure you will be in college next fall. If you happen to be lucky and you are selected from the wait list for your first-choice school, you can withdraw from your second-choice school. You'll lose your deposit, which may be $200 or $300, but it's a modest loss compared with your satisfaction.

- If you have no more acceptances, you must apply to other schools, even if you want to continue pursuing the school that's placed you on its wait list. See page 167 for advice on applying the second time around.

Step by Step

Getting to Yes

1. Find as much information as you can about the wait-list policies at the school. Call to see if the admissions office will tell you:

- If they rank the wait list.
- If so, where you are on it.
- How many students they've accepted in the last couple of years from the wait list (if they won't tell you, *The College Board College Handbook* has a table listing the number of students accepted from the wait lists of nearly 300 schools).
- An estimate of what your chances are (keep in mind that the person you speak with really may not be able to give you an answer on this, so don't be too pushy; most decisions are made by committee).

2. If you decide to continue your quest, write a letter telling the school how much you are still interested in attending.

3. If you have any new accomplishments that will enhance your application, let the college know—if your grades went up dramatically or you retook the SAT and made a huge leap in scores or won honors or awards, let them know.

4. Some colleges now have a deadline for letting people on the wait list know if they will be accepted. Find out what it is.

5. In the meantime, proceed with your second-choice application. Remember that some schools take very few students from the wait list, so never count on it. Apply for housing, accept financial aid, and assume you will be going to your second-choice school. Who knows; you may enjoy it immensely.

january admissions

Starting in winter instead of fall

A January admission is a solid acceptance. It just means that the college, for reasons of space in most cases, wants you to start next year in January, rather than this September.

This can make you really crazy if it's your first-choice school. Everyone envisions themselves moving into the residence hall in early fall, saying good-bye to their tearful parents, happily jumping into the general chaos of the opening days of school. So it can be hard to put off your dreams for college for another few months.

If you've been admitted to other schools, you have the option of going elsewhere. But if this is your first choice—or your only choice—January admission is not as bad as it may seem at first. Some colleges have so many January admits that they have an organized orientation for them. Find out what sort of assistance you can expect as a midyear student.

As this form of admittance is becoming more common, the colleges themselves are beginning to help students find good ways to spend their fall semester. Some students participate in special travel programs abroad, for example. So instead of going directly from your senior year and a couple of summer months right into the college grind, you may have the chance to travel a bit.

Of course, you'll have to pay for the program, but isn't it starting to sound a little better? Find out if the admissions office has suggestions for the fall.

ASK THE EXPERTS

What does the term "deferred admissions" mean?

Some students who have been accepted for college feel the need for some time off before beginning. This may be the result of financial constraints (you may need to earn some more money) or simply because you feel a little burnt out and need to do something else besides school for a while (travel, do community service, or whatever). There are good and bad reasons to defer, however, so be honest with yourself about your motives. Don't let yourself become permanently distracted from school.

How do I go about asking to defer admission?

Try asking the college to defer the offer of admission for a year or a semester. Some colleges will, some won't. For those that will, you'll almost certainly need to resubmit your financial aid application (everyone has to do that every year), but you may be able to preserve some of the scholarships. Generally, you must still submit a deposit and cannot take courses for credit during the time of your deferral.

FIRST PERSON DISASTER STORY

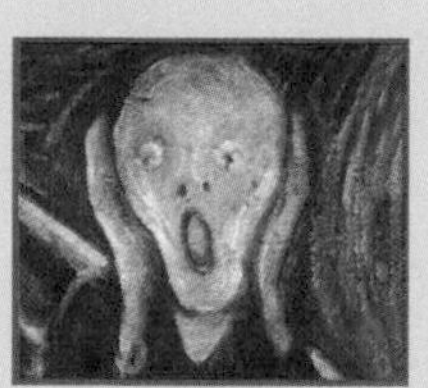

Senior Slump

When I learned in December that I was accepted by the school I had always wanted to go to, I was thrilled. I began celebrating and took the rest of the year off. I had worked so hard getting great grades in the hardest classes, preparing for the entrance exams, filling out all those college application forms, writing the essays, visiting campuses, keeping up with the debate club, and doing volunteer work that I felt I deserved to coast until the end of the year. But I goofed off so much that my grades tanked. I had no idea that college admissions decisions are conditional. In other words, if your grades fall off steeply in the senior year, even in the second semester, they could actually revoke your acceptance, which is what happened to me. It took a lot of convincing and letters to appeal that decision. The admissions office relented, and said I could attend. But the pressure is on: I have to earn certain grades in my first year. Take it from me: Avoid slacking off.

—Cris T., Arlington, Texas

now what do I do?

Answers to common questions

Help! I have three acceptances and I'm having a hard time deciding among them. Are there any Web resources that will help me compare colleges?

Yes, several. Some help you compare financial aid offers (see page 156). But there are also sites that will help you compare a variety of characteristics. Try the College Board's College Search, which gives you a side-by-side comparison of up to three colleges at a time (**www.collegeboard.com**, click on "finding the right college," then "side-by-side comparison"). The Princeton Review's site (**www.review.com**) also has a college-compare feature.

How can I survive my last semester of high school?

It's hard, with so much focus on getting into college. But take the advice of that old cliché and remember to stop and smell the roses right now. While you do have to work hard in high school, you don't have to schedule yourself up so much that you have no free time, no good times, and no rest. Remember that there are always competing pressures throughout life, and you might as well start figuring out now what your values are and where to draw the line. If you can find a sane balance throughout high school between work and play, you may not be so tempted to crash during that last fleeting semester.

Is there anything else I can be doing now to get ready for college?

College may seem like a long time in the future when you accept an offer in the spring, but many colleges are scheduling orientations in the middle of the summer these days. You'll want to start thinking about what to take to your dorm, getting in touch with your roommate, figuring out your budget, travel logistics, and even your schedule, because you may be given some information on preregistration.

If I don't start college in the fall after my senior year, how can I finish in four years?

If you've taken AP or IB exams, you may have earned enough advanced standing so that you can still graduate as you expected, in June. You will do four years of work in three and a half. On the other hand, many students take six years to finish. Finishing in four may not be overwhelmingly important.

I've been rejected from all my choices and am too depressed to start applying again. What can I do?

If all else fails, there's always the option of a local community college. While it may not be the college experience you anticipated, it will get you started, save you money, and you can transfer from there to a four-year school.

Now where do I go?

CONTACTS

College Confidential
www.collegeconfidential.com/college_admissions/admission_rejection.htm
Handling college rejection.

About's Private School
www.privateschool.about.com/library/weekly/aa030600.htm
Dealing with rejections and acceptances.

The College Board
www.collegeboard.com/finding/
Comparing colleges.

PUBLICATIONS

Getting In: Inside the College Admissions Process
By William Henry Paul and Bill Paul

Looking Beyond the Ivy League: Finding the College That's Right for You
By Loren Pope

The Insider's Guide to the Colleges 2002
By the staff of the Yale *Daily News*

chapter 9

What should I do if I'm feeling overwhelmed?
Check out page 192

hello freshman

leaving home

Sweet sorrow and new beginnings

Leaving home for college is a major life event—an exciting and somewhat scary first step into your adult life. Find it a little overwhelming? That's natural. Don't worry. College freshmen across campus and around the country are feeling the same way. College is a transition, one made easier if you keep a few basics in mind.

- Most colleges work hard at fostering a sense of community and smoothing your transition into campus life.

- Attend orientation. From these events to dorm parties, and from resident advisors to class advisors, you'll have all sorts of help in finding your way around, making friends, and becoming used to a new environment.

- Sure, you'll feel homesick. The first few weeks, even the first few months, of the freshman year are disorienting. This will pass as you make new friends and develop new routines. Remember that everyone around you feels the same way. Keep as busy as possible. Adjustment comes gradually. By the end of your freshman year you'll be surprised at how sorry you are to go home for the summer break.

- Remember that this is your time to explore, grow, and be the person you always wanted to be.

Adjusting to College Life

■ Take advantage of every program the college offers to help you adjust to your new life.

■ Go to orientation. No matter how boring the events may seem, they will get you out of your room and help you meet other students, as well as key administrators. Plus you will gain important information at these events, about everything from campus security to registration.

■ Attend dorm meetings. Get to know your **resident advisor** (**RA**), usually an upperclass student who supervises your dorm. He or she can answer a million questions and become a friendly face in a sea of strangers.

■ Find a map of the campus and surrounding area and explore your new environment. (Keep in mind any security precautions.) Check out what there is to do for fun. Invite potential friends to go along with you.

■ Go to your classes, no matter how tempting it might be to skip them.

■ Join clubs and check out the various activities and groups. Work as part of the crew on a theater production. Write for the school paper. These are all great ways to find friends with common interests, whether it's climbing mountains, playing in a rock band, or writing poetry—even if you don't pursue these activities for all four years.

■ Don't feel guilty about leaving your parents. It's your time to become independent.

an overview

Finding yourself, finding the cafeteria

Besides the emotional side of settling into college life, you will have practical issues. Here is a beginner's guide to what will come up.

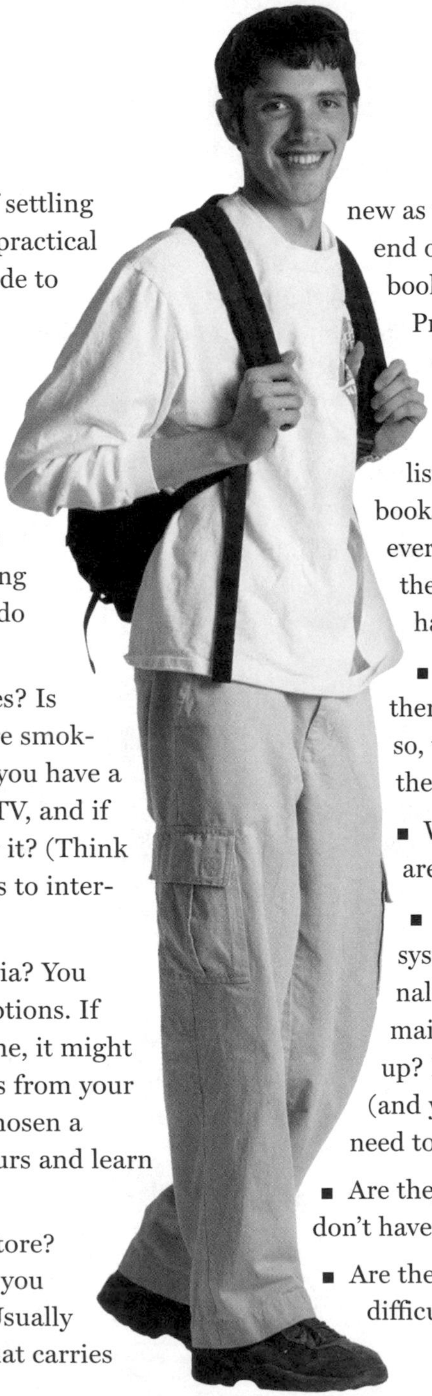

▪ How, when, and where to register for courses.

▪ Who is your **academic advisor?** (The person who approves your course schedule and makes sure you are fulfilling all your requirements.) When do you meet this person?

▪ What are the dormitory rules? Is there a visitor policy? Are there smoking or noise restrictions? Can you have a microwave? Do you get cable TV, and if so what do you have to pay for it? (Think hard about this one, as it tends to interfere with studying.)

▪ Where is the nearest cafeteria? You may have several meal-plan options. If you haven't already selected one, it might be a good idea to get a few tips from your resident advisor. If you have chosen a plan, find out the cafeteria hours and learn how your plan works.

▪ Where is the campus bookstore? Once you register for courses, you will have to purchase books. Usually the school has its own store that carries new as well as used textbooks. At the end of the semester you can sell your books back to offset your costs. Professors usually distribute a list of their required textbooks on the first day of class. Sometimes the bookstores also have the lists. The stores often have the books beforehand, so if you can, make every effort to buy your books before the first day so you'll know you'll have them.

▪ What banks are nearby? Are there cash machines on campus? If so, where? Can you cash checks at the bookstore?

▪ Where is the library, and what are its hours?

▪ How does the campus computer system work? Where are the terminals? Will you open your own e-mail account? If so, how is that set up? If you have your own computer (and you should, if possible), you'll need to get it hooked up.

▪ Are there computers available if you don't have your own?

▪ Are there tutorial centers for help with difficult subjects?

Freshman Orientation

Some colleges require freshmen to arrive on campus a few days, or even a week, ahead of the upperclassmen for a series of events called Freshman Orientation. Others schedule orientation during the summer, and many include parents.

Use this time to start making friends and find out what you need to know so you are ready to roll when classes start. Security officials will give you valuable information about which areas surrounding the school are safe, what to do if you find yourself in trouble, and if and when transportation is available around campus. Housing officials will relate important details about dorm life, such as where to do your laundry and pick up your mail.

You will meet faculty members and deans, find out about majors and course offerings, and even hear about plans for the college's future. There will also be social events, just for fun and to meet other students. Attend all these events and you'll have taken a big step toward becoming organized, comfortable, and ready for a successful year.

registration

Surviving class selection

Mention the word "registration" to most college students and be ready for groans and rolling eyes. **Registration** is the process of signing up for your classes each term. Colleges have varying procedures to do this. To their credit, many have made an effort to take some of the pain out of the process.

Still, long lines and a certain amount of frustration are practically a tradition at many schools, so don't be surprised if you encounter these evil twins.

Before you hit the campus you may receive both a course catalog, which describes all the classes offered at the college, and a schedule of when these courses will be held. While the huge catalog will be filled with enticing options, you will have some restrictions, or at least guidelines, on what you can take. (Some colleges take care of registration during summer orientation—this makes it much easier, because you can meet with an advisor and have your schedule set up ahead of the crush.) Here's what to do before you register.

- Find out how many courses, points, or units represent a full load for each term. You need to sign up for the required number of points each term to graduate on time and receive your full financial aid award.
- Consult with your academic advisor. Your advisor may have to sign off on your schedule and will make sure you are fulfilling your requirements so that you graduate in your desired two or four years. If you have questions, call and ask for help.
- Understand that there are entry-level courses (called **prerequisites**) which you usually have to take before you can take higher-level courses. Sometimes these classes have hundreds of students.

■ Find out about overall course requirements. Most colleges have **general education requirements.** All this means is that you have to take a certain number of courses in three or four broad areas, usually the humanities, social sciences, and math or the physical sciences, in addition to a number of courses in your major, to earn a degree. There may also be a language requirement.

■ Start thinking (but at this point only thinking) about a major. Generally, students fulfill their requirements in the first two years, declare a major at the end of the sophomore or beginning of the junior year, and take courses in their major in the junior and senior years.

Step by Step

Planning Your Schedule

In order to work out your schedule you need a weekly calendar and a pencil, along with the listing of courses, times, and dates.

1. Think about how you want your week to look. Do you want a four-day week? If so, avoid classes on Monday or Friday. However, this will probably mean you have a lot of classes the other days. Can you handle that? Are you a late riser? If so, try not to schedule too many early morning classes. (You may not be able to avoid them all.)

2. Prioritize the courses you need the most, write them in on the given days and times, and see if they all fit without overlap. If two are offered at the same time, you'll have to give up one of them this time around.

3. Mix up the level of difficulty. Especially as a first-year student you need to make sure not to overburden yourself.

4. Have backup plans. Just when you have the perfect schedule worked out, you may go to register and find that half the classes you want are already full. So arrive with plenty of alternatives.

dorm life

Hello, I'll be living with you

What life will be like in a dormitory or residence hall is probably the biggest question for college-bound students.

You will receive a list of the campus housing options for freshmen in the mail, along with a form to select your preferences. This package usually comes shortly after the college receives your acceptance and deposit. You may be offered a choice of coed or not, quiet dorms, or other possibilities. If you visited the campus, you may already know what you prefer. Keep in mind that on some campuses certain dorms cost more than others. Send this form back immediately for a shot at your first choice.

Your roommate will be the big question mark. While it's great if you and your roommate become pals, the most important thing is to coexist peacefully. Some basic tips will help.

- Be a good roommate yourself. Is playing your stereo interfering with your roommate's studying? Is it O.K. to borrow a pen? Be respectful, and with any luck, your roommate or suitemates will be respectful of you. If not, discuss it.

- First impressions can be misleading. It takes time to get to know someone, so give him or her a chance.

- Keep your sense of humor. Don't sweat the small stuff.

- Work out the practicalities. If you have a refrigerator, you need rules. Some of the worst fights are about refrigerator issues. Can you eat only what you buy? Or can you eat something as long as you replace it? How often will you stock up? Can your guest have that last soda your roommate bought? Also, cleaning up: Do you care if there is laundry on the floor? Can you borrow clothes?

- What about visitors? Plan a way to give each other some privacy.

Dorm Norms

What to Pack

The college will probably provide you with a list of things to bring. If the college gives you your roommate's name and number ahead of time, you may want to call and discuss this. Do you both need to bring a major sound system? On the other hand, do you share well?

The Resident Advisor

Most dorms come with a resident advisor (RA), often one on each floor. This upperclass student has a ready ear for you and provides advice and mediation when there are problems.

Regulations

Find out your dorm's rules, such as those about smoking, alcohol, drugs, and fire hazards. Many dorms conduct random searches of rooms.

Computers

Every college student needs a computer. You may be able to purchase one from the college, new or used, at a good price and know that it will be compatible with campus systems. Or you may bring your own. Most schools have terminals for students' use stationed around campus, but it's tough to do all your work this way. As for printers, this is another item to discuss with your roommate ahead of time. If you can settle on one printer that's compatible with both of your computers, why take up precious space with two?

Roommate Advice

If you've really tried to get along with your roommate but find it simply impossible, you may be able to switch. See your RA for advice. Colleges try hard to encourage students to learn to work out their differences, so they may make you wait until the second semester before changing rooms.

managing your time

Find a balance

While you probably juggled a complicated schedule in high school, college may be the first time you have to figure it all out yourself and stick to it, without teachers or parents keeping track.

Learning to manage time can make the difference between succeeding or failing at college.

Skipping classes is a big temptation at college, especially because some professors don't even take attendance. But are you getting away with something, or just throwing all your hard work (not to mention money) down the drain? (If you are sick, it's up to you to see your professor and find someone to give you a copy of the notes. In college no one will tell you this. You have to take the initiative.)

At the same time, have fun. Neither the total party animals nor the completely obsessed, nail-biting worker bees have the full college experience, and both are self-destructive in their own ways. Find a balance between work and play. This is a challenge in managing your time that will become increasingly important in your life.

Step by Step

Getting Organized

1. Buy a personal organizer with a weekly calendar and use it. Among the many brands, Day Timer makes a special one for students. If you're a tech wiz, you may prefer a nifty handheld organizer.

2. Just as in high school, write in all your homework, short- and long-term assignments, holidays, deadlines, and so on. Figure out when you need to have finished outlines and drafts and put those dates in too. Enter all the phone numbers and addresses of friends and family into your organizer before you leave home.

3. Make a big copy of your schedule and post it on your bulletin board, next to the college calendar.

4. If you have a map of the campus, put that up too. Know how to get to your classes before the first day they're held.

5. Make sure you write down the names of all your professors; the exact title, time, and location of each course; the location of your professors' offices; and their office hours. Keep the same information about your academic advisor.

6. Buy all your supplies before your classes start. Your professors will expect you to be ready to take notes on day one.

managing your money

Learning to live on a budget

Most high school students have at least some experience managing money. But in college you need to be totally in charge. If you are the type who saves, plans a budget, and generally sticks to it, the adjustment may be easy. But if money slips like water through your fingers and you find yourself out of cash halfway through the semester, your parents may not be willing or able to bail you out.

To start setting a budget, determine what your expenses will be and how much you have to spend. But how can you estimate what your expenses will be?

Start by breaking this down into necessities, like textbooks, supplies that you will need for your dorm room, money for transportation home, and extra money for discretionary items like movies, snacks, and so forth. Add up these amounts to see your total expenses.

Now determine if you and your parents can come up with this amount of money. If not, you will have to cut your expenses or find new sources of funds, like getting a job.

How to Manage Your Money

Bank accounts Most college students open a bank account. Banks near colleges usually offer good deals for college students, so shop around. Another option is to open an account with your parents' bank so that they can easily make deposits into your account. Find out what cash machines are on campus, and make sure your bank card is compatible with them so you can avoid extra fees.

Credit cards You've probably already received several credit card offers. Some credit cards, like Visa and MasterCard, that allow you to make purchases up front without cash, can be useful in establishing a good credit rating, and may be handy in an emergency. But be careful before you sign on. Credit cards can land you quickly in debt you can't handle.

If you pay just the minimum monthly payment on your bill, it may take years to pay back what you owe. In the meantime, you'll have spent almost twice what your purchases originally cost. Your credit rating is what landlords, employers, and banks check when deciding whether to rent to you, hire you, or lend you money.

Charge cards Similar to credit cards, charge cards are issued by individual stores or companies. They are a little less risky because you are required to pay off the full balance you charge each month. You don't pay high rates of interest, but you do pay an annual fee. American Express is an example. If you can't pay back the money you've charged, you lose your ability to use the card, collection agencies may come after you, and your credit history is tarnished.

Debit cards Some bank cards that you use at cash machines also function as electronic checks. This is great, because you don't have to carry around large amounts of cash, and when you want to purchase something the money is deducted directly from your checking account.

making friends

Reaching out, joining in

Beyond your roommate or suitemates, you'll find a campus full of interesting people, among them potential friends.

- Join clubs, which will link you up with people who have common interests, whether it's chess, Greek culture, pan-African music, the environment, homelessness, gay and lesbian support groups, or others.
- Play sports—from organized soccer to informal Frisbee, your team members will likely become friends.
- Go to college events—film screenings, dorm meetings, parties, big games, theater department productions—where you can start meeting other people.
- Talk to people before and after class.

Like you, every first-year student wants to make friends.

FIRST PERSON SUCCESS STORY

From Roommates to Friends

I was really nervous about meeting my roommate. I've always had my own room, and I wasn't looking forward to giving up my privacy, especially to a complete stranger! But while our personalities were really different, we turned out to be compatible in the way we lived. We liked a lot of the same music and even though she slept later than I did, we never seemed to get in each other's way. Although I studied more, I benefited from the fact that she was more sociable, because she brought lots of people into our room and we all became friends.

—Carol D., Raleigh, North Carolina

Sororities and Fraternities

Some campuses offer a built-in option for making friends—sororities and fraternities known as the Greek system. This national network of campus clubs is a big part of the social life at some colleges, a marginal part at others, and banned outright at others.

- Where they are established, Greek clubs provide housing, a continual source of fellowship, social activities (somewhat mandatory), and definitely a communal feeling. The Greek system's reputation has been tarnished in recent years because of initiation rites, called hazing, that have resulted in injury and death to some students.

- At some campuses, fraternity parties and beer kegs seem inextricably linked. Still, defenders point out that on other campuses, fraternities and sororities (some of whom ban alcohol) play an important, positive role in student life, lead to life-long friendships, and are embraced by their administrations.

- Those interested in joining a club must go through something called **rush,** a period during freshman year (in the fall at some schools, spring at others) when potential members apply and are interviewed. If your parent was a member you will be known as a legacy and will probably be invited to join your parent's fraternity or sorority. But don't jump at the first offer—find out about all your options.

Before Joining, Ask Yourself:

- Do I want to limit my friendships by being part of an exclusive club? Will I make as many friends by joining as I would in any case?

- What is the Greek culture on this campus? Is it likely to help me become a better student and person, or lead me into trouble academically or socially?

- Have I explored all the clubs and decided which to join? (You'll spend most of your time socializing with other members, so make sure you like the people and the general atmosphere.)

- Will I face initiation? (If you are asked to do anything dangerous or are pressured to break rules, don't. This is a club you don't want to join.)

- Will I be moving into Greek housing? (If so, check out the facilities and living arrangements.) Can I live without a lot of privacy?

taking time out

Leaving college, graduating later

While most people think of college as four years, it can take longer. Perhaps for economic, personal, or medical reasons, some people need to take a break and then go back. In fact, many colleges now list the percentages of students who complete their degree in six years.

Most colleges permit you to withdraw voluntarily for a certain period of time and then return to finish school. The key is that last part: to return and finish. If you are in school and are struggling under some sort of burden, you probably won't do as well in your studies as you would otherwise. In that case, you may be wise to take a year or two off to sort out the problem, or take fewer classes. Far better to take advantage of this official option than simply to drop out and never finish.

If you feel you need to take some time off, what do you do? As always, one of the keys to succeeding in college is to communicate. People who run colleges are real people. They've taken a chance on you by accepting you, and they want you to succeed. So talk to them and plan a painless exit. Colleges have a variety of voluntary withdrawal policies, from a leave of absence for travel or work to medical leave. The specifics vary from school to school. Go see your advisor or class dean and explain your circumstances. Ideally, you want to do this before you start a new semester. Together you can plan how and when you leave and return.

ASK THE EXPERTS

What sorts of reasons would a college consider good enough to grant a withdrawal?

While policies vary, lots of reasons can gain you a voluntary withdrawal. You may feel you just need a different kind of experience, like travel or community service for a year (many colleges are sympathetic to that) or you may be needed at home because of a family crisis. You may be experiencing economic hardship and need to work and save some money before continuing your studies. If you are sick, you can request a medical leave of absence.

How does voluntary withdrawal work? Do I have to reapply for admission?

Again, policies vary, and you'll have to ask for the specifics of your school from your advisor or dean, but in general you are usually allowed to withdraw for a specific reason for a limited period of time, say for up to two years. (The school may also insist upon a minimum period of time for your absence, such as a year.) When you wish to be readmitted you may, in some cases, be required to demonstrate in some way that you have dealt with the reasons for your withdrawal. If you were ill, for example, and took a medical leave of absence, you may have to submit documentation that you are now well enough to attend school. However, you do not have to go through the entire admissions process again as if you had never attended the school.

Is there any downside to voluntary withdrawal?

It's possible that you will lose your housing. And, since financial aid is awarded on a yearly basis, you will have to reapply. There is no guarantee that you will receive the same financial aid package you did previously. Also, depending on when you leave, you can be charged fees as well as lose your tuition or semester deposit.

now what do I do?

Answers to common questions

What happens if I get sick?

Find out where the health center is and put its number on your wall. Find out how the health services work. What do you do when you are sick, just show up at the center, or call for an appointment? Do you have to pay for visits? Know what sort of health coverage you have, either through your parents or the school. Carry an insurance card in your wallet or make a photocopy of your parents' card. Finally, memorize your Social Security number. If you ever need to see a doctor, especially off campus, this is a standard bit of info you'll need. You'll be asked your Social Security number about a zillion times in your life, so you might as well learn it now.

How can I continue my workout regime at college?

Every college has at least one fitness center for you to use, and often they'll have facilities far better than anything you've used before. So locate the gym and check out its equipment. Find the hours and policy for use. Plan a fitness program for yourself.

What should I do if I'm feeling overwhelmed?

College can be lots of fun, but it can also be stressful. If you or someone you know show signs of overload, it is extremely important to seek help. Speak to an RA or, better yet, to someone at the health center. Many colleges offer psychological services. If they don't have such people on staff, they will refer you. Don't be ashamed to ask for help. You may just need someone to talk to or advice about handling all the demands you're juggling. Or you may be suffering from depression, a real, and unfortunately all too common, illness that can require treatment. Don't tell yourself you should be able to handle it. After all, do you "handle" a strep throat? If these feelings persist, you should alert your parents.

What if someone I know seems troubled?

You may be reluctant to interfere. But you do someone a favor by finding them help when they may not be able to ask for it themselves. If someone has a serious problem, speak to your RA immediately. There's no need to try to handle this one yourself.

Should I bring my bike to school?

Bikes can be great for getting around, but first find out where you can keep it securely. If it's far from your dorm, that may defeat the purpose.

Should I listen to rumors about professors when I register for classes?

Definitely! You shouldn't take just one student's word, but if you hear from several that a professor is especially warm, intellectually stimulating, and takes a personal interest in her students, that's someone to aim for, assuming the course is of interest and fulfills some of your requirements. If someone is a dragon, bored by his students, or disorganized, why waste your time and money? But the situation can be more complicated—there may be professors who have a reputation as unkind or arrogant yet deliver totally brilliant lectures that are the whole reason you went to college.

When will I know who my roommate is?

Most colleges send you the name and contact information of your roommate before school starts. It's probably a good idea to call and introduce yourself. If you had summer orientation, you may have already met.

Now where do I go?

CONTACTS

Campusaccess.com
www.campusaccess.com
Campus life site.

The Princeton Review
www.princetonreview.com/college/research/articleIdex.asp#life
Articles on college life.

StudentNow
www.studentnow.com
Good college life site.

myFootpath
www.myfootpath.com/CollegeLife/PrestonDormLife.asp
Tips on living with a roommate.

PUBLICATIONS

The Everything College Survival Book
By Jason R. Rich

Bringing Home the Laundry: Effective Parenting for College and Beyond
By Janis Brody

Letting Go: A Parents' Guide to Understanding the College Years
By Karen Levin Coburn

The Real Freshman Handbook: A Totally Honest Guide to Life on Campus
By Jennifer Hanson

CHAPTER 10

I have big expenses—family, bills, debts, you name it. How can I afford college?
Check out page 197

Going back to college

back to school

Finishing your degree or starting a new one

If you've secretly fantasized about getting a college education or finishing a degree you started ages ago, there's never been a better time. Did you know that 40 percent of all college students today are nontraditional students? Education for older students who are going back to school is big business these days, and many colleges are eager to recruit you.

Rather than having your worst fears realized—that you'll be the only salt-and-pepper head in your class, or the only one who can't fit into size-2 jeans—you'll find courses packed with your peers, all eager, like you, to get something more out of life. Professors also often enjoy teaching older students, who are more certain about what they want out of school and more willing to work.

You can expect informed admissions officers who can tell you about the array of options available to adults, from certificate programs to part-time and full-time degree programs, both graduate and undergraduate, to nondegree courses in a wide range of subjects. Many colleges, recognizing that adults have their own needs, offer separate admissions procedures (including transition and re-entry programs), flexible, nontraditional class scheduling, and a variety of support services tailored to adults.

So don't hesitate to start the process.

ASK THE EXPERTS

I have big expenses—family, bills, debts, you name it. How can I afford college?

Nontraditional students are eligible for most of the same federal and state education aid that helps younger college students (see chapter 7). And there are other possible sources of aid as well (see page 208 for suggestions). Investigate the subject of aid thoroughly with admissions or financial aid counselors.

How will I juggle college, my job, and my family responsibilities?

Carefully assess why you are going back to school and decide if it's an appropriate time in your life. If you are sure of your commitment, you will be better prepared for the sacrifices. It's also advisable to start out slow, with just one or two classes, and see how that works before you get in over your head.

How can I go to college when I have to work all day?

Take advantage of the flexible schedules many colleges offer, including some Saturday all-day classes. Or join the throngs of adults now getting degrees right in their homes at their computers. Maybe 3 a.m. is the only time you have for a class—if so, distance learning (an online class) is for you! (See page 206-207.)

Where can I find out more?

Two excellent online resources for anyone considering going back to college are **www.collegeispossible.com/adults/adults.htm** and **www.adultstudentcenter.com**.

Continuing Ed

Community colleges usually cater to a large adult population, offering both full degree programs and individual noncredit classes, which can include everything from flower arranging to computer programming. Large universities may have separate schools just for older students.

why now?

Choosing a new path

Before you start looking around for the right college to attend, decide what your goal is. Some people go back to school to start or change careers, or boost one that's not advancing as fast as they would like. Others are happy in their current profession but interested in more education.

▪ Did you postpone college and now are just getting around to it? If so, what is your career goal, and what sort of degree (four-year/two-year, grad/undergrad) will you need?

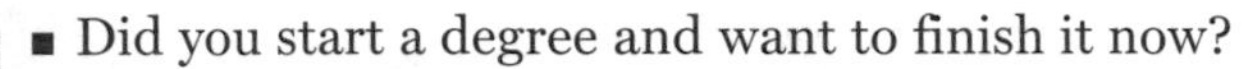

▪ Did you start a degree and want to finish it now?

▪ Do you want to change careers? If so, you may need to start from the beginning.

▪ Are you looking for a full-degree program, or would a certificate program—which can be finished more quickly—work for you!

▪ Do you have an undergraduate degree and want to go to graduate school? Or would you like a second bachelor's degree in another subject?

ASK THE EXPERTS

Where can I find out about careers I'm interested in?

Look at **www.mapping-your-future.org**. You can click on their Adult student link and from there explore everything from career planning to finding a large list of links to Web sites exploring various careers, job descriptions, and degree requirements. At **www.jobweb.com**, which also lists actual jobs, you can click on Career development for a complete guide to career planning. The site has links to assessment and aptitude tests and information on which schools offer courses in your field.

How useful are books on changing careers?

Very useful, and one in particular is indispensable—the *Occupational Outlooks Handbook, 2002–2003*. Published by the U.S. Department of Labor's Bureau of Labor Statistics, it is a massive, thorough listing of jobs, descriptions, pay scales, and working conditions—really terrific for researching careers and fun to browse through. It's available online at **www.bls.gov/oco/** or you can buy it at your bookstore. If you are really confused about the entire direction of your career and need to do a fundamental assessment, you still can't go wrong with that old favorite *What Color Is Your Parachute? A Practical Manual for Job-Hunters and Career-Changers*, by Richard Nelson Bolles, updated regularly.

Express Admissions

Do you simply need a few noncredit classes (i.e., continuing ed classes that are not part of a degree program) to upgrade your skills? If so, you can usually bypass most admissions procedures. Simply fill out a registration form, send in your check by a given deadline, and you're in. (There are exceptions: for example, some writing classes require you to submit samples of your work.)

the right program

Full time or part time

Once you've decided on the career you wish to pursue and the sort of degree required for it, you need to find the right school and program to meet your needs. You'll have to make some decisions.

- Full-time or part-time study?
- Day, night, or weekend classes?

- On-campus or external (**distance learning** or online-only) classes? Or both?
- How much time can you devote to study?
- How much money can you afford to spend, and how much financial aid can you expect?
- How long will this take to complete?

Just like any other potential college student, you'll need a good college handbook to begin searching for schools. As recommended previously, *The College Board College Handbook,* updated every year, is a good choice. It lists just about every two- and four-year college in the United States. By using its indexes, you can find schools in your area that specialize in your degree or certificate program. You may also want to consult a career college guide, like *Peterson's Guide to Career Colleges 2002.*

Finally, you can use Web sites like Princeton Review's **www.review.com** and Peterson's **www.petersons.com** to conduct searches, find valuable admissions and financial aid information, and see links to college Web sites.

Step by Step

Checking Out Colleges

1. Visit each college's Web site. Does the school offer the degree or certificate program you want? Find out if there are separate schools or programs for adults. Are part-time studies possible?

2. Once you've got some basic information, call the admissions office (you can get the number off the Web site or from your college handbook).

3. Important: Ask if they are accredited and by whom (special regional agencies determine if a college meets minimally accepted standards). Be careful about this, because there are many shady operations targeted at nontraditional students that offer quick, easy, but worthless degrees. If you have any doubts, contact your state department of education and find out if they are legit. It's your time and your money.

4. Ask if there is a separate admissions advisor for adults.

5. Ask if there are separate admissions procedures for adults. (Sometimes some tests, like the SAT, are waived, but there may be other entrance exams.)

6. Ask if there are any specific admissions requirements (special tests, prior degrees, and so on) for the program you are interested in. See if you can get credit for life experience. You may be able to take a test to skip a course whose topic you have mastered on the job.

7. Ask if there is a financial aid advisor for adults.

8. If you need support services, for example for a disability or child care, ask if they are available.

9. Ask when most classes are held (days, nights, weekends), and if distance education (page 206) is available.

10. Find some statistics on the school itself. What percentage of the students are adults?

11. Set up an interview and take a campus tour. Talk to nontraditional students and see how satisfied they are. Colleges can't guarantee you a job upon graduation (and beware of any that claim they can), but they should have ways of helping you find work in your field.

applying to colleges

Transcripts and child care

If you are applying for a degree or certificate program, much of the process of choosing and applying to schools will be the same for adults and high school seniors. (See chapters 3 and 5.) But because of the large number of adult students today and their different needs, many colleges now have separate procedures just for adults.

Many of your concerns may have to do with getting the admissions materials together. It's been a long time since you were in high school: Does your alma mater still have a copy of your transcript? You took the SAT 20 years ago, or never. What to do? These are common concerns, and colleges are used to helping adults through the process.

Depending on the school, you may find

- A different admissions application for adults, which you can obtain online or in the mail
- Special open houses for adults
- Separate admissions officers and financial aid advisors
- Separate schools
- A separate center just for adults
- Adult re-entry and transition programs
- On-site child care

There are no single standard procedures for every school. Take a look at the application and wherever you have a question or concern, ask.

Help Is Here

Depending on the circumstances, many requirements can be waived. Some colleges may require you to take an entrance exam, but this varies from school to school. If exams are required, the college may have materials to help you prepare for them. In fact, some colleges offer brush-up or transition courses if you've been away a long time. The main message is that they want your business. They will help you through the process. Everyone else is doing it. So can you!

Fast Facts: The GED

Colleges often require a high school diploma. If you didn't finish high school, you can take the GED (General Educational Development) High School Equivalency Exam.

1. You can take the exam at 3,400 U.S. locations, including schools, community colleges, and adult education centers. The tests are given year-round.

2. The GED is a mostly multiple-choice exam in five parts: writing skills (including a short essay), social studies, science, interpreting literature and the arts, and mathematics. You can take the tests all at one sitting or spread them out over several days.

3. Standard scores range from 200 to 800. You need a standard score of 400 to pass each test and an overall average of 450 for the five tests.

4. To register, call 800-626-9433 or check your local phone listings for GED testing centers.

For more information on the GED, go to the Web site of the American Council on Education (**www.acenet.edu/calec/ged**). The site offers a description of the test, answers to common questions, links to testing locations and places offering test prep for it, and information on how to understand your scores. Or call 800-626-9433.

How to Prepare

The school system or community colleges in your area may offer prep classes, and you can also prepare for the exam online and with test prep books. These include *Cracking the GED 2003* by Geoff Martz and Arco's *Everything You Need to Know to Score High on the GED* by Seymour Barasch. Kaplan, Peterson, and all the other major test prep publishers offer similar guides. Look in the reference section of your local bookstore.

degree express

Ways to speed up your education

No matter how much fun college may be, most working adults want to move their education along as quickly as possible. There are several ways to speed up getting your degree.

■ Earn credit for courses already taken. Did you take college classes elsewhere? You may be eligible for full or partial credit transfers. Ask the admissions officer.

■ Take the CLEP exams (see page 122): These are standardized, multiple-choice exams offered by the College Board, which many schools accept for college credit.

■ Take accelerated classes. These can vary from all-day Saturday classes to ones offered every weeknight. But they can be intense, so make sure you can handle the pressure!

■ Earn credit for work experience, military service, or prior learning. Sometimes classes you've taken for your job, or even your life or work experiences, can be translated into college credit.

ASK THE EXPERTS

Are you telling me I can receive credit for things I already know?

In some cases, yes. For information, check with your admissions officer and see books like *Earn College Credit for What You Know,* by Lois Lamden and Susan Simosko, and *College Credit Without Classes: How to Obtain Academic Credit for What You Already Know,* by James L. Carroll. Finally, check out the American Council on Education's College Credit Recommendation Service at **www.acenet.edu**, where you can also see information about gaining credit for military experience.

FIRST PERSON DISASTER STORY

Avoiding Overload

I couldn't stand the thought of how long it was going to take me to get my degree while working full-time, so I decided to take some accelerated classes. At first it was fine. The class met every night, and I was really psyched. I managed to do homework on the weekends and get myself out the door of my job on time. But when I signed up for the second class, it got crazy. I came down with the flu and missed a week of classes. I was so far behind! Then my job heated up and my boss started pressuring me to stay late. I had no time for my family, and the pressure was too much. I got through it, but after that I decided to slow down. It wasn't worth it. My goal is to finish college, not set some kind of speed record. Slow and steady wins the race.

—**Bennett B., Seattle, Washington**

online degrees

The campus comes to you

One of the great revolutions in college today is the rapid growth of online, or distance, education, earning a degree by using your homecomputer. Simply put, you can pursue a degree without going to a campus regularly. Be cautious and do research to be sure the school you choose is accredited.

Distance education began in the last century with home study courses, which were sent back and forth through the mail. You can still find mailed correspondence courses and some videotape courses, but distance education classes are more likely to be online. There, professors can post lectures, students can submit homework, and discussions can be held in **chat rooms,** areas online where people can have a "live" conversation using typed messages instead of their voices.

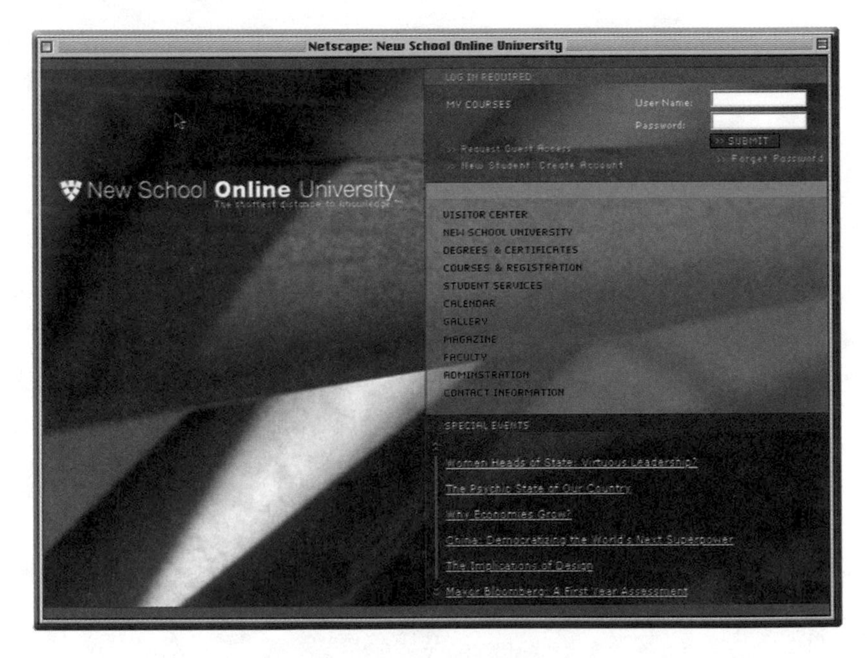

Distance education is a boon for many returning students and people with disabilities who can't find the time for regular college classes. You can even take courses online from universities in other states. Chances are that when you check out adult education classes at various colleges, you'll come across information on their distance learning programs.

ASK THE EXPERTS

How can I decide if distance learning is a good choice for me?

Distance learning is great for some people, but not for others. First, you have to have a computer and be comfortable going online and sending e-mail. You need a lot of motivation, because you make your own schedule. You have to not mind working alone. And you need to be a reasonably good writer, because that's how you communicate with your fellow classmates and teacher.

Is there any way I can try a class before paying for it?

One fun way to gain a feel for how online classes work is to go to the Web site operated by New School University's Online University (**www.dialnsa.edu**). It's a terrific source of information about how online courses work. You can even register as a guest and participate in an actual online course for a few days.

Are distance learning degrees acceptable to prospective employers?

That depends almost entirely on the quality of the college that awards it to you. You can become lost in a sea of online degree programs, so make sure yours is from a reputable, accredited institution. It's best to check out colleges in your area, even if you are going to do your degree online. You can find more information about them and go in there if you have a problem or want to actually meet your professor. Also, you can check with your current or prospective employers to see how they view online degrees. Keep in mind, however, that this is a relatively new type of degree and you may have to educate employers about it.

Where can I find a list of online college courses?

Web sites like Peterson's (**www.petersons.com**) will do a search through more than 3,000 distance learning programs. Another site to try is **www.collegedegree.com.** You'll also find several guides at your local bookstore, including a print version of Peterson's, as well as *Bears' Guide to Earning Degrees by Distance Learning*. Any good college profile book, such as the *The College Board College Handbook,* should have an index of schools offering distance learning options (in the College Board guide the index is called "Internet delivered courses available" and is broken down by state).

financial aid for older students

What's out there for you?

Financial aid isn't just for teenagers. If you are a returning older student, you are eligible for most of the same aid, and in a few cases you might have a few extra resources to draw on. Sources you should consider include the following.

Federal and state aid programs Adults are eligible for the same federal and state aid programs, from Pell Grants to Stafford Loans, that enable high school students to attend college. You will have to fill out the **FAFSA** (Free Application for Federal Student Aid) and attend a school with proper accreditation. To review all the basic information about FAFSA and various types of aid, both federal and state, see chapter 7.

Your employer Many companies will pick up the cost of some of your college education. Some stipulations usually apply—often the courses need to be related to your career within the company.

Your union If you belong to a union or someone in your family does, you may be eligible for some tuition assistance. Check with your union representative.

Military benefits If you are a veteran or current member of the armed forces, you may be eligible for college financial aid. There are some restrictions, though. Check out **www.gibill.va.gov** (click on "eligibility and certification").

Education IRA withdrawals Make penalty-free withdrawals for education expenses. Check with your accountant for details.

Private scholarships Some scholarships are restricted to returning older students. You can try a scholarship search and see what turns up. For information on how to do this, see page 138 and take advantage of free scholarship searches on **www.fastweb.com**.

ASK THE EXPERTS

Should I consider a community college, to cut costs?

These are the best bargains in education. Many adults earn their degrees at community colleges. You will find rock-bottom tuition, part-time programs, night classes, and support services for adults, including those returning to school after many years. If you want a diploma from a higher-status school, you could begin here and transfer later.

Can I cut costs by finishing faster?

You certainly can, but rather than work yourself to the bone, see about gaining credit for classes or work you've already done, or by taking an exam (CLEP) on the subject. Every credit awarded before you start is one you don't have to pay for with your money and time. See page 204.

I own a house. Can't I just take out a loan against it?

Yes, you probably can. You also may be able to borrow against your life insurance policy or retirement plans such as a Keogh or a 401(k). Check with your accountant.

See a Pro

If you need financial aid, make sure you check with a financial aid advisor at your college. While you should investigate as much as possible on your own, they are professionals and are masters of the details. They will also know about any special scholarships the college may offer for adults.

now what do I do?

Answers to common questions

I want to go back to college, but I have a 2-year-old, and no one to help me, day or night. What can I do?

Many colleges have special adult student services, which can range from admissions and career counseling to on-campus day care. Check around and see which colleges near you are most supportive of your needs. Adult services can also include personal counseling, financial aid counseling, women's services, veterans' counseling, and even alcohol- and substance-abuse counseling.

I just want to take a few computer classes to get up to date. Do I have to go through all the admissions procedures you describe?

No. Most of what's described in this chapter refers to degree or certificate programs. If you just want to take a few noncredit classes, you can usually just fill out a registration form, write them a check, mail it in on time, and you're in. Sometimes there may be a prerequisite (courses you have to take first) and you may have to submit some samples (for, say, a poetry or drawing workshop). Noncredit courses are usually offered through schools of "continuing education." If you can't access their course descriptions online, call and request a catalog. All the admissions procedures and requirements are spelled out clearly. Many adults add a little spark to their life or career through these sorts of classes.

Distance learning sounds like the way for me to gain a college degree, but I'm not very computer savvy. What should I do?

The short answer is to get your computer skills up to snuff. To do that, you may have to find the time to take one continuing ed course on campus in basic computer skills. You will be doing yourself a huge favor, since computer skills are essential to most jobs today and for navigating the modern world in general. Once you have the hang of it, you'll see it's not really very complicated and you'll have access to a whole new world. Then you can go ahead and try one distance learning class to see how you like it. At that point, you'll be ready to take the plunge.

Aren't there educational tax credits I can claim?

Yes! Don't forget about the Hope Scholarship Credit and Lifetime Learning Credits. (See page 144 for a full description.) These let you take a credit of up to $4,500 on your taxes. But check the requirements before you file—you have to attend college at least half-time for the Hope credit. You can check the details about tax credits, IRA withdrawals, and more from the Internal Revenue's Web site **www.irs.gov**.

Now where do I go?

CONTACTS

CollegeNET
www.collegenet.com
Internet admissions applications for college and university programs.

College Is Possible
www.collegeispossible.com/adults/adults.htm
Great college prep resource.

Norman Davies Group
www.adultstudentcenter.com
Information and guidance on returning to college.

PUBLICATIONS

Princeton Review's Never Too Late to Learn: The Adult Student's Guide to College
By Vicky Phillips

Adults in College: A Survival Guide for Nontraditional Students
By Wanda Schindley

Back to School: A College Guide for Adults
By Laverne L. Ludden

Cracking the GED 2003
By Geoff Martz

Arco's Everything You Need to Know to Score High on the GED
By Seymour Barasch

glossary

Academic advisor A college faculty member or administrator who is responsible for approving your class plan each semester and giving you general advice to keep you on track toward your degree.

Academic calendar A schedule for the college year, consisting of semesters, terms, or quarters. These may include fall, spring, summer, and winter. Some schools operate on trimesters. Others, especially small liberal arts colleges, may have various shorter sessions interspersed.

Accelerated degree Any program of study that allows you to earn your college degree in a shorter than usual time.

Accreditation Recognition by a regional or national accrediting body that a college meets basic quality standards. Any college you contemplate attending should be accredited.

ACT (Formerly known as American College Testing.) One of the two most commonly required college entrance exams.

Advanced Placement (AP) courses Rigorous high school courses offered through the **College Board** in more than 30 subjects. Passing AP exams with high enough scores can result in credit or advanced standing in many colleges.

Articulation agreement A formal agreement between colleges regulating transfer policies, including the amount of transfer credit awarded for courses at each institution.

Associate degree A degree awarded after two years of full-time college study or its equivalent.

Bachelor's (or baccalaureate) degree A degree awarded after the completion of a course of undergraduate study (theoretically completed in four years). The two most common are the B.A. (bachelor of arts) and the B.S. (bachelor of science).

Candidates reply date Under **regular admissions** procedures, most colleges agree to May 1 as the deadline by which students must accept an offer of admission.

Class rank Based upon your grades, where you stand in relation to the rest of your class.

CLEP (College-Level Examination Program) Tests offered by the **College Board** that can result in college credit at many schools.

COA (Cost of attendance) This amount is calculated by each college, based upon tuition, room and board, and other expenses. It's one of the numbers used to determine your financial aid package.

College The next stage of higher education after high school. The term on its own usually refers to four-year schools granting a bachelor's degree, but there are two-year colleges (community, junior, and upper division) as well.

College Board The nonprofit organization that administers the **SAT, SAT II, CLEP,** and **AP** exams. Its Web site (**www.collegeboard.com**) is an essential stop for any student contemplating college.

College Scholarship Service (CSS) Profile Also known as the Profile, this is a financial aid form required by some selective or private colleges when you apply for financial aid.

Common Application A standardized admissions application accepted by many colleges. The Common Application, where accepted, can save applicants an enormous amount of time.

Community college Two-year government-subsidized colleges with low tuition and often open admissions.

Commuter A student who lives off-campus. Some schools (particularly community colleges) are commuter schools with no housing, so everyone has to live off-campus.

Credit Units awarded for courses completed in college; colleges require varying numbers of credits to graduate. Tuition is often calculated upon a set price per credit.

Deferred admissions A policy by which some colleges allow students who have been accepted, to postpone attendance for a semester or a year.

Distance learning College programs that allow students to take courses or entire degrees off-campus. Distance learning can include videotapes, correspondence, and other means of communication, but these days it most often means taking classes online.

Early action An admissions alternative at some schools through which students can apply early and get an early answer from the college. Unlike **early decision** programs, the student is not bound to accept an early action offer, and can continue to apply to other schools.

Early decision An admissions option at some schools, where the student applies early to one favorite school and agrees that, if admitted, he or she will accept the offer as binding and will withdraw all other applications.

EFC (Expected family contribution) The amount a family is expected to contribute to the cost of attending college; the EFC is determined based upon a formula after you file the **FAFSA** (see below). Some colleges have their own methodology or depend upon a different form (the **CSS Profile**) to compute the EFC.

FAO (Financial aid officer) These are people at the college who can guide you through the ins and outs of applying for aid.

FAFSA (Free Application for Federal Student Aid) A financial aid application required by most colleges, and one that must be filed by anyone who wishes to receive any government financial aid.

Federal methodology This is the formula the folks from **FAFSA** use to determine your **EFC** (expected family contribution), which they report to you on your **SAR** (student aid report). In other words, this determines your eligibility for federal funds and other aid. Some colleges use a different technique, known as the institutional methodology, which takes other family assets into account.

Financial aid package The package offered to you by the college that works out how you will pay for your education. It typically consists of various combinations of grants, loans, and/or work study, and the total, in the best-case scenario, makes up the difference between the **COA** (cost of attendance) and your **EFC** (expected family contribution). Financial aid packages may meet your full need, but these days some do not.

GED The high school equivalency exam accepted by most colleges for those applicants who did not complete high school.

Gift aid Another term for grants or scholarships; in other words, money you don't have to pay back.

Grade point average (GPA) Your grade point average is an overall assessment of your academic record. It is most commonly calculated according to a 4-point system based upon your grades and the number of course or credit hours for each course.

Graduate school After college, where you earn a bachelor's degree, the next stage of higher education is graduate school, where you can earn either a master's degree (usually an M.A. or M.S.) or with more years of study, a doctoral degree (the Ph.D.).

Grants Financial aid awards based upon need that do not have to be repaid. Federal Pell Grants are an example.

Greek organizations Fraternities and sororities, usually exclusively male or female, that function like clubs on campus, offering social activities and, frequently, housing to members.

Guidance counselor A great person to know, a high school advisor responsible for helping you gain entry into college.

Historically Black Colleges and Universities (HBCU) A group of schools whose main mission is the education of African-American students; they were originally founded to meet the higher education needs of students denied admission elsewhere because of segregation.

Honors courses Rigorous high school courses open only to students who demonstrate high academic achievement.

Hope scholarship credit A tax credit of up to $1,500 a year for the first two years of college.

IB (International Baccalaureate) A demanding degree program offered in some high schools that prepares students for international colleges. IB courses can also be used to earn advanced standing or credit at some U.S. colleges.

Institutional methodology This differs from the **federal methodology** in calculating your **EFC** (expected family contribution) and eligibility for some other forms of aid; colleges that use it usually requires you to complete the **CSS Profile** form in addition to the **FAFSA.**

Ivy League A group of eight distinguished colleges in the Northeast: Brown, Columbia, Cornell, Dartmouth, Harvard, Princeton, the University of Pennsylvania, and Yale.

Junior college While the term is sometimes used interchangeably with community college, a junior college is a two-year college that may also be private, expensive, residential, and have regular (as opposed to open) admissions requirements.

Legacy An applicant with a relative who attended the same school; also refers to an applicant to a sorority or fraternity whose parent was a member.

Lifetime learning credit Previously a tax credit of up to $1,000, the credit is up to $2,000 as of January 1, 2003.

Loans Part of your financial aid package, this is money you have to pay back. Depending on the source and type of loan, the terms vary. Some education loans are for students, some for their parents.

Major In college, after a student fulfills general course requirements, she or he then takes several courses in one concentrated area, which is the major.

Minor Similar to a **major** but involving fewer courses in the concentrated area of study. A student may declare a minor in addition to a major but not instead of a major.

Need We all know what need is. But when it comes to financial aid, it has a special meaning. When calculating your financial aid package, colleges deduct your **EFC** (expected family contribution) from the **COA** (cost of attendance) and what's left is your "need." So your need varies depending on the difference in cost among the colleges you apply to. Colleges try to meet your need through a package combining grants and scholarships, loans, and work-study.

Need-aware or need-sensitive admissions A policy where a school considers your ability to pay when making an admissions decision. Some schools with a need-aware policy say they only use it for borderline admissions decisions.

Need-blind admissions An admissions policy where a school does not consider whether a student can afford the school when deciding to admit that student.

Open admissions An admissions policy where a college admits anyone who applies, without regard to their academic record. Community colleges often have open admissions.

Orientation A series of programs and events that colleges offer to freshmen and transfer students, either in the summer or a few days before school begins, to help them get settled.

Pell Grants A federal grant program for low-income students.

Perkins Loan Program Need-based higher education loans for students from low-income families; the program is underwritten by a variety of sources, including the federal government and the colleges themselves.

PLAN A preparation test for the **ACT,** offered in some schools during the sophomore year.

PLUS loans (Parent Loans for Undergraduate Students) A program of higher education loans for parents, with a capped interest rate of 9%. They are not based upon need and are available to anyone with a good credit history.

Profile See **College Scholarship Service Profile** above.

PSAT/NMSQT (Preliminary SAT/National Merit Scholarship Qualifying Test) A practice exam to prepare students for the **SAT**; it's also used to determine who qualifies for National Merit Scholarships.

Professional school A general term for schools after college that prepare you to work in professions such as law or medicine.

RA (Resident Advisor) The person, usually an upperclassman, who organizes activities and deals with problems in your dorm.

Regular admissions The traditional college admissions procedure: Students must submit all materials by a given date (usually in January or February); all applicants are notified of the college's admissions decisions at the same time in the spring; and all students have until May 1 to accept an offer.

Rolling admissions An admissions policy that allows students to apply at any time, as long as there are openings. Students get an admissions decision shortly (often within two or three weeks) after all the materials have been received.

SAR See **Student Aid Report.**

Scholarships Like grants, scholarships are gift money that you don't have to pay back. Scholarships are not always based upon need but may be based upon achievement or other criteria.

SAT The most commonly required and well-known of the college admissions exams, administered by the **College Board.**

SAT II One-hour subject tests required by some colleges in addition to the **SAT** or **ACT.**

SEOG (Supplemental Educational Opportunity Grant Program) A federal grant program for low-income students.

Selective Service Federal aid comes from Uncle Sam, boys, and unless you register with the Selective Service when you turn 18, you will not be eligible for any financial aid.

SSIG (State Student Incentive Grants) A variety of state grant programs that are encouraged by federal incentives.

Stafford Loans A federal student loan program; Subsidized Stafford Loans are based upon need, and their interest is covered by the government while you are in school.

SAR (Student Aid Report) The form you get back from the U.S. Department of Education after you file the **FAFSA.** It summarizes your family finances and calculates your **EFC** (expected family contribution).

Transfer program Students sometimes choose to switch schools. Transfer programs allow students to carry with them the credit they have earned for courses at their first school.

Tuition The cost for a full course load at college for one year. Sometimes, especially in the media, the term is used interchangeably with the "total cost" for a year of college, and this can be very misleading.

Undergraduate A college student (as opposed to someone attending graduate school, who is known as a graduate student).

Upper division college Some two-year colleges, often career or technical training schools, offer only the junior and senior year. You must attend another college for the first two years of study.

University A large institution composed of both graduate and undergraduate schools, and usually some professional schools.

Wait list A list of students a college will admit if and when there are any openings.

Work study A federal program that helps you pay for college by providing you with a part-time campus job where you work an estimated 10-20 hours per week.

index

A

B

C

D

E

F

G

H

I

J

L

M

N